PRAIRIE DOGS

PRAIRIE DOGS

A Wildlife Handbook

Kim Long

Johnson Books
BOULDER

Published by Johnson Books, a division of Johnson Publishing Company, 1880 South 57th Court, Boulder, Colorado 80301.
EMAIL books@jpcolorado.com

9 8 7 6 5 4 3 2 1

Series cover design: Margaret Donharl
Cover illustration: Kim Long

All illustrations by the author unless otherwise indicated.

Library of Congress Cataloging-in-Publication Data
    Long, Kim.
        Prairie dogs: a wildlife handbook / Kim Long
            p. cm. — (Johnson nature series)
        Includes bibliographical references and index.
        ISBN 1-55566-270-6 (pbk. : alk. paper)
        1. Prairie dogs. I. Title. II. Series: Long, Kim. Johnson nature series

Printed in the United States by
Johnson Printing
1880 South 57th Court
Boulder, Colorado 80301

CONTENTS

ACKNOWLEDGMENTS

Bill Alther, The Denver Museum of Nature and Science
Dr. Randall Lockwood, Humane Society of the U.S.
Gregory McNamee
Kathleen Cain
Greg Goodrich
Pat Wagner and Leif Smith
Cassandra Leoncini, Crow Canyon Archaeological Center
The Bloomsbury Review
Denver Public Library
Western History Department/Denver Public Library
The Stephen H. Hart Library/The Colorado Historical Society
Norlin Library/University of Colorado
Auraria Library/Metropolitan State College
William E. Morgan Library/Colorado State University
Penrose Library/University of Denver
The Tattered Cover Bookstore

INTRODUCTION

When western explorers first encountered prairie dogs, their reaction was typically one of awe. Not because of the physical attributes of this North American rodent — as a relative of ground squirrels and marmots, it had a familiar appearance — but because of the sheer numbers visible. Existing in the hundreds of millions, their colonies were spread throughout most of the territory west of the Missouri River. That such "lowly" rodents could accomplish this massive display of group living made a significant impression.

The admiration of prairie dogs continued through the early years of western settlement — the last half of the 1800s — when most of the traffic through this territory was heading to the West Coast. Pioneers trundling across this vast expanse of land relished the scenery but found it of little value except for harboring beaver and bison, representing commercial opportunities. The soil itself — protected by a tough mat of grasses and grass roots that thwarted plows — was too difficult to farm. As long as this land was "useless," the prairie dogs that inhabited it were ignored.

Yet as plow designs improved — and the press of population from the East made these lands more attractive — the millions of prairie acres previously left alone for the use of native cultures and wildlife quickly turned into a valuable commodity. As much as war characterized the conflicts between the Indian tribes blocking this expansion, farmers and ranchers declared war on prairie dogs, competing for valuable cattle fodder, not to mention the land occupied by their burrows and thus unavailable for commercial use.

Prairie dogs, to this day, remain to many an enemy of progress and are systematically shot and poisoned, even though their ranks are already reduced to only a few percent of their original numbers. Some species are so decimated that their survival is in question. But like the beaver, bison, and gray wolf before them — previously decimated species with a new-found public support — this status is not necessarily permanent. Information is one key to this reversal, a wider exposure to the unique nature of this original prairie dweller.

PRAIRIE DOG MYTHOLOGY

"The prairie dog is, in fact, one of the curiosities of the Far West, about which travellers delight to tell marvelous tales, endowing him at times with something of the politic and social habits of a rational being, and giving him systems of civil government and domestic economy, almost equal to what they used to bestow upon the beaver."

— Washington Irving (1835, *A Tour on the Prairies*)

Among the numerous types of animals found in the West, the prairie dog may have been greater in numbers than others, but it had much less impact as a mythical symbol. While coyotes, eagles, and rabbits, among others, figure prominently in Native American stories, rituals, and religions, prairie dogs show up much less often, and for some tribes, not at all. In most cases, these underground-dwelling rodents appear in myths only as secondary characters, serving as food or foil for other, more colorful animals.

In one Navajo tale, a young boy who was hungry hatched a plan to catch prairie dogs for his dinner. He walked up to a prairie dog village carrying a large empty sack. The prairie dogs were curious because they recognized the boy but couldn't figure out what he was carrying in the sack. "What do you have in the sack?" they asked him, to which he replied, "I'm carrying a sack of dance songs." This caused the curious prairie dogs to demand he sing them one of the songs. The boy agreed, but only as long as the prairie dogs formed a circle around him and closed their eyes.

The prairie dogs made a circle, closed their eyes, and the boy began singing. But at the same time, he pulled a stick out of the sack and began whacking the unsuspecting prairie dogs on their heads, trying to kill all of them to satisfy his appetite. He killed all of the animals except one, a little girl prairie dog who had opened her eyes

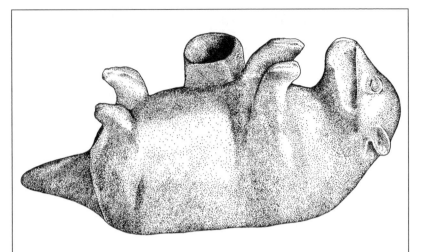

Traditional clay vessel in the shape of a prairie dog. This pottery style comes from an area near Colima, Mexico, and was the hallmark of a culture centered there from circa 100 BC to 250 AD.

slightly to see what was going on. Frightened, she ran away, and to this day, every prairie dog now alive is related to her.

Among the Jicarilla Apache, there is the myth of the Fox and Prairie Dog. Fox, paying a visit to Prairie Dog, was cordially invited inside. Playing the part of the generous host, Prairie Dog placed four sticks, each about one foot long, in the ashes of the fire. Pulling them out of the ashes, the sticks turned into roasted meat, which Prairie Dog offered to Fox for his dinner. In return, Fox invited Prairie Dog to visit his own home, upon which occasion Fox attempted to duplicate the generosity of Prairie Dog. He also placed four sticks in the fire, but instead of turning into roasted meat they burned up instead. Prairie Dog lectured Fox that he should not attempt to perform this kind of feat and that he, Prairie Dog, could do so only because he was a medicine man and was able to transform wood into meat. Saying this, Prairie Dog then proceeded to demonstrate, again preparing a meal of roasted meat from sticks placed in the fire.

A traditional tale from the Lakota tells of the Prairie Dog people who quit dancing. Worried about this inactivity, Owl came to the prairie dogs and made a speech about bravery, hoping to inspire them to dance again. But the prairie dogs did not respond, and did not dance. Then Badger, hearing Owl's speech, also made a speech about bravery, yet the prairie dogs remained still. Skunk also tried to inspire the motionless prairie dogs, but his speech about bravery did not work either. After this, Rabbit spoke and then Prairie Chicken, but their speeches did not help. And then Buffalo came up to the prairie dogs and made a speech, but he, too, had no luck in inspiring them.

Disappointed in their efforts, the animals held a meeting and decided to form societies that would represent how brave each type

SONG OF THE PRAIRIE DOGS

Once the prairie dogs and wildcats were all white. There was a prairie-dog man who wanted a wildcat woman to run away with him. At first she did not like him, but afterwards she ran away with him. Her mother did not want her to marry the prairie dog because he did not hunt. Her mother wanted her to marry the magpie, who hunted and got rabbits and other animals. So the mother went and took her daughter away from the prairie dog and gave her to the magpie, who gave his mother-in-law everything that he got in the hunt. They lived up the mountain. The mother-in-law told the prairie dog that he was of no use because he lived in the ground.

A traditional song from the Northern Ute culture, as published in the *Smithsonian Institute Ethnology Bureau Bulletin 75* (1922, Washington, D.C.)

of animal was. The societies held meetings in which they made speeches to inspire bravery, and when the Owls made their speech, the prairie dogs finally began to dance. Even today, when prairie dogs run from burrow to burrow, the Owl makes its distinctive call to inspire them to run bravely.

In Pawnee mythology, there is the story of the boy who turned into a prairie dog. In this tale, the boy, whose name was Black-Eyes, was attracted to a girl, who he followed and talked to as she went to dip water from the creek. Even though the girl scolded him, Black-Eyes persisted in following her, until she turned to him and said, "Boy, I want you to know that I do not care for you. I can never marry you and I do not want you to talk to me any more." Heartbroken, the boy went home and told his mother of his sorrow, then taking his bow and arrow, left the village and traveled east.

Outside of the village, he began to cry and his tears fell on the ground. Going further, he entered the Prairie Dog town, where he spotted a young girl standing. He went to her and soon they lived together in her lodge beneath the ground. Black-Eyes' mother, missing him, went in search of her son and spotted his footprints leading to the east. She also saw the marks of his tears on the ground.

She came to the Prairie Dog town where the footprints ended next to a big hole. There she began to cry and her tears flowed for several days. During the day, she saw two prairie dogs come out of the hole. Falling asleep, she had a dream in which there was a beautiful young woman who was very short.

The little woman spoke to the mother in the dream, telling her "Woman, you must not cry any more for your son, for he is married to me. The girls of your people refused to marry him. He came to our village; I took him in and married him. We are living together and are happy. There is but one way by which you can get your son back. Your son has forgotten all about your people. Go to your home. In his quiver there is one black arrow that the boy made himself and of which he thought a great deal. Bring that arrow, and lay it near the hole. You must then lie down."

Awakening, the mother followed the advice from the dream,

4

Prairie dogs and other small animals were sometimes used by Native American tribes to make bags for tobacco or medicine. This traditional Sioux tobacco bag was made from the whole skin of a prairie dog and was used as a tobacco pouch. The pouch is decorated with porcupine quill embroidery and was carried with the head hanging from the waist, suspended from a belt or sash. The bag was used to carry tobacco (probably kinnikinic, a native plant that was sometimes referred to as "Indian tobacco"), a tobacco pipe, and the equipment needed to start a fire, usually flint, fire-steel, and touchwood.

This illustration, from a picture titled "Indian Pouches for K'nich-K'neck," is by George Catlin (1796–1873), from *The Manners, Customs, and Condition of the North American Indians*, written and published by Catlin in 1841. Reproduced with permission from the collection of the Colorado Historical Society, Denver, Colorado.

COYOTE SINGS FOR THE PRAIRIE DOGS

In the mountains Old Coyote Mother and Father were living. Old Man Coyote had a little drum and he sat above the road and beat the drum and sang,

> Look out! Look out!
> Coyote is going to hit you
> On the back, on the back.

Lots of prairie dogs came running. They cried, "Dear me, grandfather. How beautifully you sing! Sing it again and we'll dance to it." Coyote began to beat his drum again and the prairie dogs made a circle and stood out to dance. Coyote sang again,

> Look out! Look out!
> Coyote is going to hit you
> On the back, on the back.

They stepped in time to the song. "Grandfather, sing it again. It is such fun to dance to your song." They danced and danced.

Grandmother Coyote called, "Come on, grandfather. Let me sing a while for them." The prairie dogs said to Grandfather Coyote, "You sing so nice, sing again." "No, your grandmother is in a hurry." "We know she is calling you, but please sing some more. You sing such a beautiful song. Sing it again and we can learn that song."

A traditional tale from the Cochiti culture, as published in *Tales of the Cochiti Indians,* by Ruth Benedict (Smithsonian Institute Ethnology Bureau Bulletin 98, 1931, Washington, D.C.)

returning to the Prairie Dog town with the black arrow, and she placed it near the hole where the footsteps ended. When her son emerged from the hole, he spotted the arrow. Grabbing it, he turned into a boy again. Speaking to his mother, he told her they could go home, but he must take his wife with them, for she was pregnant with his child. Calling to his wife, the pregnant female prairie dog followed after the son and his mother as they walked away. When they came to their home, she rolled in the dust and turned into a woman.

Many years later, the now-grown-up Black-Eyes met a girl near the creek, but did not reply when she spoke to him. She asked for an explanation and he told her that she had scolded him long ago. After apologizing for her rudeness, the two went into the brush and were together. Later, Black-Eyes told his wife what had happened, and she took her children and went back to her home, where she and her children turned into prairie dogs. From that time on, Black-Eyes had bad luck.

The Comanche have a traditional tale about the Coyote and the Skunk. The two animals were hungry and created a scheme to get something to eat. Skunk entered the prairie dog village and lay on the ground, pretending to be dead. Coyote also then entered the village and spotted several prairie dogs playing near their burrows near where Skunk lay on the ground. Calling to them, Coyote encouraged all the prairie dogs to come out of their burrows and hold a dance of celebration to rejoice in the death of their enemy. He told the prairie dogs to plug their burrows behind them and dance in a circle with their eyes closed.

As they began to dance, Coyote killed one of the prairie dogs and called to the others to open their eyes. "Look," he told them, "this one opened his eyes and he died. Everyone should close their eyes and start dancing again, but if you open your eyes, you, too, will die."

As the prairie dogs danced with their eyes closed, Coyote killed them one by one. But one prairie dog grew suspicious and peeked,

PRAIRIE DOG DAVE

In the early days of the settlement of Kansas, a man named David Morrow arrived in Hays City, seeking to make a living hunting buffalo. Although Morrow succeeded in earning money selling buffalo meat, sometimes there was a meat surplus and he had to find other ways to generate cash.

According to local legend, one of his schemes was to capture and tame young prairie dogs. He would then stand on the platform where passenger trains arrived, introducing newcomers to the friendly nature of the little tamed animals. He sold the prairie dogs for five dollars each and generated enough demand to turn this into a regular business.

Finding it hard work to flood prairie dog burrows with water in order to capture new animals, he invented a new system. He would place a barrel filled with sand over the entrance to a burrow; the sand would flow into the burrow, forcing a prairie dog to dig its way upward, where it would be trapped in the then-empty barrel.

As his business boomed, Morrow became known as *Prairie Dog Dave*, but competition from others soon forced the price for the captured animals down from five dollars to as low as twenty-five cents, eventually putting him out of business. He spent the rest of his life in a variety of occupations — for a long period of time, he was a lawman in Dodge City — but his nickname stuck with him to the end.

An illustration captioned "The Prairie Dog or Wish-Ton-Wish (*Spermóphilus Ludoviciánus*)" from *Popular Natural History*, by Rev. J.G. Wood, published in 1885.

seeing what Coyote was up to. He called to the others in alarm, and they all ran to their burrows, removing the plugs and rushing to safety.

From the Zuñi pueblo comes the traditional folk tale of the Prairie Dog Land, where the Prairie Dogs and their priest, Burrowing Owl, lived. During one rainy summer, the residents of a large village prospered because of the abundance of fresh plants. But the rain kept coming, making the people wet and uncomfortable even as they grew fat from the plentiful food. Rain collected in puddles and then deeper pools, covering the food plants, and eventually, the Prairie Dog people began to lose weight and grow hungry.

Alarmed at their predicament, some of them stood on their mounds and called out in their shrill voices, "Wek wek — wek wek — wek wek!," summoning all the people to a council at the base of the mountain where Burrowing Owl had his home. They complained about the never-ending rain and came up with many ideas

Prairie dogs were a popular subject in early books about the western United States. This line engraving was reproduced in *Natural History of Western Wild Animals*, by David W. Cartwright, published in 1875.

about how to make it stop, but all were futile. Finally, a wise old Prairie Dog suggested that they take the problem to their grandfather, Burrowing Owl, and the people sent him there as a messenger. Climbing the mountain, the old Prairie Dog begged for help. In reply, Burrowing Owl stated that he would fast and meditate for four days in order to come up with a solution.

The next morning, Burrowing Owl captured a foul-smelling beetle, a stink bug well known for the nasty, over-powering odor of its defensive spray, which he promised not to hurt. Instead, he had his wife offer it large quantities of beans to eat, a particular type of bean well known for the gas it produced during digestion. The foul-smelling beetle ate bowl after bowl of the beans, until he was stuffed and could eat no more.

Meanwhile, Burrowing Owl prepared a round piece of buckskin, making it into the form of a pouch. He warned the foul-smelling beetle that although the beans he had just eaten created discomfort, he was likely to get even more uncomfortable as the gas from the beans expanded inside of him.

If the beetle wanted to avoid further consequences from his gluttony, Burrowing Owl suggested he should stick his head into the buckskin pouch and have his stomach squeezed to expel the excess gas. The foul-smelling beetle found this an acceptable idea and allowed the sack to be tied around his head. Burrowing Owl then gently squeezed the beetle, whose girth decreased at the same time as the bag filled up with escaping wind. Relieved of the pressure from the gas, the beetle thanked Burrowing Owl for the meal and departed. Left behind was the buckskin bag, stuffed to capacity with a potent gas, a little bag of powerful medicine.

When the fourth day arrived, the rain continued to fall. It was then that Burrowing Owl took the pouch of gas to the mound in front of his home and holding it high in the air, whacked it with a stick. Clouds, thunder, and lightning began to drift away, fleeing from the foul odor driven from the bag. He hit the pouch again, releasing more gas and a small clearing appeared in the sky. Again and again he whacked the bag, expelling all of the foul-smelling gas and driving all the clouds from the sky, making it as clear as noon on a summer day during a drought. So strong was the all-penetrating odor that even the Rain Gods themselves had to withdraw their forces.

All the Prairie dogs gathered around the mountain and sitting up on their hind legs, shouted in joy in their shrill voices, "Wek wek — wek wek — wek wek!," praising their priest, Grandfather Burrowing Owl. Since that day, prairie dogs and burrowing owls have been good friends and these owls think the best place to live and raise their families is in the holes dug by the prairie dogs.

PRAIRIE DOG POWER

"The title of Prairie Dog has been given to this animal on account of the sharp yelping sounds which it is in the habit of uttering, and which have some resemblance to the barking of a very small and very peevish lap-dog."

— Reverend J.G. Wood (1885, *Popular Natural History*)

Although not as prominent as other animals in Native American rituals, prairie dogs still made an occasional appearance. In the Fox culture, for instance, a special ceremony was held whenever camp was to be moved to new ground. This ceremony lasted four days and four nights; during the days, ceremonial dancing took place in which symbolic items were carried or worn, including sashes made of prairie dog skins. Among other plains tribes, members on occasion dressed as prairie dogs to represent friendly animals during ritual dances.

Among the Apsarkoke, society was traditionally divided into families, led by members who fasted and were inspired by various animal spirits. These groups included Those of the Weasel, Those of the Otter, Those of the Real Tobacco, Those of the Blackbird, and Those of the Prairie-dog.

The Cheyenne had a traditional ceremony during which special animal songs were sung. These included the songs of Otter, Hell-diver, Muskrat, Mink, Woman Beaver, Child Beaver, Marmot, Buffalo, Dog, Fish, Lynx, and Prairie Dog. While singing, articles representing each animal were carried four times around the ceremonial fire by a woman.

Zuñi Indians hold burrowing owls in high regard, considering these birds to be important benefactors. They are referred to as "priests of prairie dogs." And among the Hopi, burrowing owls are thought to have the power to make seeds sprout and to keep fires burning; they are also keepers of the dead. Traditional Navajo sand paintings, an important part of some healing ceremonies, sometimes included stylized images of prairie dogs, burrowing owls, and black-footed ferrets.

The Jicarilla Apache associated the prairie dog with rain, able to lead people in thirst to sources of water. Navajos also saw a relationship between prairie dogs and water. They believed that all such burrowing animals served an important function for the earth by creating "breathing tubes," which released moisture-rich air, helping to create rain.

Early western settlers also adopted some myths about prairie dogs. Since it was believed that these rodents could not survive without water, which was rarely present around their villages on the surface, their burrows must be connected to underground aquifers or springs. In a quest for this hidden bounty, pioneers sometimes dug deep into the earth where prairie dog villages were found. It was not until the 1900s that scientists completely dismissed this myth by excavating burrow systems, which laid entirely above water-tight barriers of underground rock.

An illustration from *The Western World, Picturesque Sketches of Nature and Natural History in Northern and Central America*, by William H.G. Kingston, published in 1884.

PRAIRIE DOGS AS FOOD

"But of all the prairie animals, by far the most curious, and by no means the least celebrated, is the little prairie dog. This singular quadraped is but little larger than a common squirrel, its body being nearly a foot long with a tail of three or four inches."

— Josiah Gregg (1845, *Commerce of the Prairies*)

Aplentiful resource, prairie dogs were hunted as food by many Indian cultures throughout their range. Excavations of ancient Anasazi ruins have unearthed large numbers of prairie dog bones, indicating that these rodents provided a significant source of food in some areas, possibly even more than larger game animals such as antelope or deer. Other western tribes also depended on prairie dogs as a source of protein, but to varying degrees.

Because prairie dogs are active throughout the year, at least through most of their range, these animals may have provided an important source of meat protein during parts of the year when buffalo and other primary sources of meat were scarce. They were also much more plentiful, generating a greater supply than the shifting populations of larger game animals.

For some tribes, prairie dogs were hunted with bow and arrow. Western explorers remarked on the skill of these hunters at picking off distant animals with such "primitive weapons," even while their own firearms proved less than adequate for the task. But shooting was not the only way to bag a prairie dog. Indians were known to flood prairie dog burrows to force animals to the surface for capture.

Among the southwestern pueblo cultures, water for this purpose was sometimes diverted from irrigation ditches; sporadic rainstorms also provided an opportunity to gain the upper hand on these elusive creatures.

One trick reported for this kind of attack was to plug a burrow entrance with grass and manure. An earthen wall would then be constructed around the burrow and filled with water. When the plug was yanked from the hole, the water would rush in and drive out the occupants before they had time to escape through secondary tunnels.

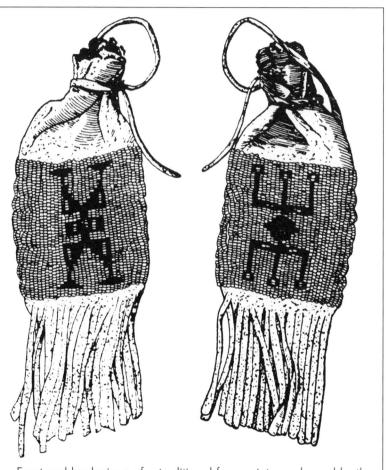

Front and back views of a traditional face paint pouch used by the Arapahoe tribe. The design represents both a prairie dog and a saddle bag. Illustration from *The Arapahoe*, by Alfred L. Kroeber, published in 1902 in the *Bulletin of the American Museum of Natural History*.

Another trick used for this quarry comes from the Navajo. They would use a piece of mica, found locally in some parts of the southwest, to reflect sunlight into the opening of a burrow. As a prairie dog emerged, the light was bright enough to blind it temporarily, permitting an easier shot from the bow of a waiting hunter. Other Indians used snares made of horse hair placed at burrow entrances, and emerging animals trapped themselves. Deadfalls could also be employed. These devices were rocks or slabs of stones delicately propped up with sticks. Prairie dogs that brushed against one of the supports would be killed by the crushing weight of the falling stone.

When used as food, prairie dogs were most often baked or roasted. Open fires were the most common form of heat but some tribes also depended on the heat of glowing coals or pre-heated rocks.

While Native Americans may have found prairie dogs a welcome source of meat, this practice was not often shared by western explorers and settlers. To most western palates, the taste of these fatty rodents was often described as gamey and unappetizing, unlike the meat of elk and bison, which was relished. But when other sources of food were scarce, pioneers were willing to take advantage of this resource.

PRAIRIE DOG NAMES

"The general impression of those persons who have never seen the 'Prairie Dog' called by the French Canadians 'petit chien,' would be far from correct in respect to this little animal, should they incline to consider it as a small 'dog.' It was probably only owing to the sort of yelp, chip, chip, chip, uttered by these marmots, that they were called Prairie Dogs, for they do not resemble the genus Canis much more than does a common gray squirrel!"

— Reverend John Bachman (1851, *Audubon's Mammals*)

nglish-speaking pioneers and explorers dubbed these chattering rodents "prairie dogs" specifically because the sound they made seemed very similar to that of domesticated dogs. Zebulon Pike, one of the first western explorers to venture into the range of these creatures, called them *Wishtonwish*, a name used by Indian tribes in the area of what is now Kansas. But because they were found within the original Louisiana Territory and resembled marmots, some people called them Louisiana marmots; they were also referred to as prairie marmots, prairie squirrels, barking squirrels, and prairie barkers. Other common names included the Missouri prairie dog, the Missouri barking squirrel, and the mound yapper.

To Spanish explorers, they were "perro de la pradera" or "perrito de la pradera" (literally, "dog of the prairie" and "little dog of the prairie"). These days, they may also be referred to as the "pero llaneros" or "perrito de las llanero"; *llanero* is another Spanish word for prairie. More specifically, this becomes "perrito de las llanero norteamericano."

In some areas of the West, Spanish-speakers also used the word *tusa*, thought to be borrowed from one of the native cultures of the region, as another traditional term. In the state of Chihuahua, where prairie dogs are traditionally found, they are also sometimes just called "perritos" or more specifically, "perrillos de Chihuahua."

Illustration from *Natural History: A Manual of Zoölogy*, by Sanborn Tenney, published in 1873.

French explorers in the high plains called them "petit chiens," or little dogs. German visitors dubbed them "prairiehunde."

The first prairie dogs to be examined by zoologists were obtained by the Lewis and Clark expedition between 1804 and 1806. Because the region that these explorers were trekking across was called the Louisiana Territory, the first scientific name given to the animals was *Arctomys ludovicianus*. The genus name *Arctomys* was borrowed from that used for marmots, a close relative of prairie dogs; the species name *ludovicianus* is the latinized version of Louis, the French king for whom the territory was named. George Ord (1781–1866), an American naturalist, is credited with making this designation in 1815.

In 1817, Constantine Samuel Rafinesque (1783–1840), also a naturalist, decided that these animals deserved their own genus to differentiate them from the marmots. For this purpose, he coined the term *Cynomys*. This scientific word was generated from two Greek words, *kyn* for "dog" and *mys* for "mouse." For several decades, there was confusion about which of the two designations should be used but the conflict was resolved in 1858, when Spencer

SIGN LANGUAGE

Among some North American Indians, difficulties translating between tribal languages could be overcome by using sign language, a system of signals that was more or less consistent across large parts of the country. To make the sign for *prairie dog*, the hands were first held together in front, palms down, and swept out and down, indicating a mound. Then, the right hand was pushed up with the first finger extended, representing the prairie dog emerging from a burrow.

A variation on this sign replaces the sign for mound with the one for hole. In this case, the two hands were held together with the thumbs and fingers forming a circle.

Yet another variation started with the right hand held down and to the right of the body, suggesting the short height of the animal. Then, both hands were used to make the sign for hole. Finally, the left hand was held, partially closed, in front of the body while the closed right hand was raised. When the right hand just cleared the left hand, the thumb was snapped up and down against the index finger, symbolizing the chattering of a prairie dog.

F. Baird (1823–1887), a naturalist who became the head of the Smithsonian Institute, supported the recognition of two distinct species, the black-tailed prairie dog and the white-tailed prairie dog, each of which was given its own scientific name. In 1916, Ned Hollister (1876–1924) proposed that prairie dogs in North America belonged to one genus, with two subgenera and a total of seven species and subspecies.

AMERICAN INDIAN LANGUAGES

Because prairie dogs are only found in a limited area of the American West, not every Native American culture was familiar with them. Tribes on the East and West coasts, for example, did not have words for this animal in their vocabularies.

ACOMA — nï tᵤ

AKIMA O'ODHAM (PIMA) — shesheliki

ALABAMA — lapcho

APACHE — ch'osh dit'ógé

BLACKFOOT — kómmoyo'kstsiikinakimm

CATAWBA — andotaksoso

CHEROKEE — igodi ehi gili

CHEYENNE — ononevoneške

CHICKSAW — saalnkona

CHOCTAW — lupchu

CREE — pasowahkesîs
paskwâwatimosis

CREEK-MUSKOGEE — hvyakpo-efv

CROW — achepabecha

DAKOTA SIOUX — pizpíza
wum-DOO-sh'kah-nah

DELAWARE — huppeechk

HOPI — tukya

KALISPEL (FLATHEAD) — heuhenemúl
es-heuemi

KIOWA — kahimhi

LAKOTA SIOUX — pizpiza
waglula

MINGO — u'nöwöegta'

MOHAWK — otsi'nonwahnhe:ta

MOKI — dirk'quar

MUSKOKEE — semakwiku

NAVAJO — dlóó
ni'ch'osh
glo-un

ONONDAGA — otschinúngwa

OSAGE — moⁿthiⁿ' xo-dse

POTAWATOMI — kwukse'

TAOS — ke'oo una

TEPA — tenpi

TOHONO O'ODHAM (PAPAGO) — sheliki
tehhr

UTE — tûn-uck
túc-e

WESTERN APACHE — nii'lleezhé

ZUNI — k'usha
tusah
tusa

Currently, zoologists limit prairie dogs to five species, keeping them subdivided into the previous two subgenera. The white-tailed prairie dog was dubbed *Cynomys leucurus*, with the species name deriving from the Greek word *leukos*, for "white" or "light," referring to its distinguishing tail color. The species name for the Gunnison's prairie dog is *gunnisoni*, a derivation of the place name Gunnison, located in west-central Colorado. The Gunnison River, Mount Gunnison, the town of Gunnison, and the county of Gunnison were all named after Captain John W. Gunnison, a government surveyor who camped in the area in 1853 while exploring for a potential transcontinental railroad route.

When first encountered by westerners, some naturalists believed that prairie dogs were marmots, an animal they were familiar with in Europe. This illustration is captioned "The Prairie-Marmot," from *The New Natural History*, by Richard Lydekker, published in 1890.

Among the five prairie dog species, the Utah species is the smallest and thus this animal received the species name *parvidens*, originating with the Latin word parvus, meaning "small." The Mexican prairie dog, like the Gunnison's, has its species name matched to the region where it is found, *mexicanus*.

PRAIRIE DOG SPOTS

In the United States, "prairie dog" appears as a name on many natural landscape features. Geographical locations in the United States named for the prairie dog number 63. Among the geographic features — both natural and man-made — that include the words "prairie dog" are ...

2 bays	1 lake
3 canyons	1 park
6 canals	1 archaeological site
1 coulee (dry creek)	1 river
12 creeks	2 schools
2 dams	2 springs
2 draws	12 tanks and reservoirs
1 wildlife area	3 townships
2 flats	1 trading post
2 hills	1 valley
1 knoll	3 windmills

PRAIRIE DOG SPECIES

SIZE COMPARISON

Prairie dogs of the same species in the same geographic region tend to be similar in size. Variation in size among adults is often linked to latitude, with larger body sizes in the warmer, southern, portions of their range. In late summer and fall, adults will also be fatter as their bodies store extra food for the coming winter months. Females of all species, as well as young adults (less than one year old) are smaller than adult males.

BLACK-TAILED PRAIRIE DOG
MEXICAN PRAIRIE DOG

The largest species and similar in size. Tails up to two inches longer than other species.

WHITE-TAILED PRAIRIE DOG
GUNNISON PRAIRIE DOG
UTAH PRAIRIE DOG

Similar in size. Tails shorter than other species.

ROCK SQUIRREL

One of several species of ground squirrels that share territory with prairie dogs. Smaller in size, with longer tails.

BODY FEATURES

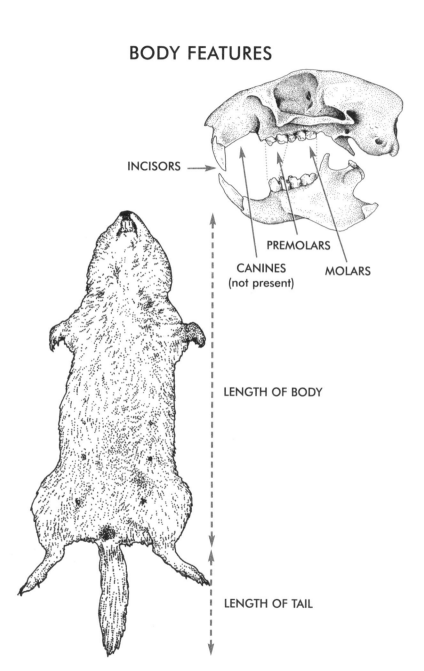

INCISORS →

PREMOLARS

CANINES
(not present)

MOLARS

LENGTH OF BODY

LENGTH OF TAIL

BLACK-TAILED PRAIRIE DOG

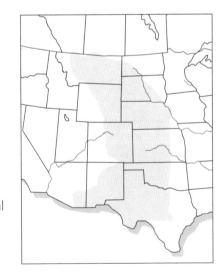

RANGE

Approximate normal
range of species.

VITAL STATISTICS

NAME	**Black-tailed prairie dog** *Cynomys ludovicianus* **SPANISH** perrito de las praderas
DESCRIPTION	Solid, bulky body with short legs and relatively small head, small ears, short tail. Color tan or beige to brown, may have pinkish tinge; lighter on sides and belly. Tail features distinctive black tip. Fur short and even in summer, long and rough in winter. Body shape typically sleeker and thinner in winter and spring; fuller to fat in late summer and fall. Albino and melanistic (dark) phases known, but rare. Males larger than females.
COMPARISON	Only species other than Mexican prairie dog to have black-tipped tail. Only species found in its range.
TOTAL LENGTH	14–17 inches (36–43 cm) **TAIL LENGTH** 2¾–4½ inches (7.2–11.7 cm)
WEIGHT	31¾–48 oz. (900–1,360 gm)
TEETH	22 teeth total: incisors 1/1; canines 0/0; premolars 2/1; molars 3/3
HABITAT	Shortgrass prairies, non-rocky soil, altitude between 2,300–5,570 feet (700–1,700 meters).
RANGE	Missouri River west to the Rocky Mountains, extreme southern Canada south to northern Mexico.
ACTIVITY	Diurnal; does not hibernate but may be inactive during periods of cold or extreme weather. Sexually mature in 2nd year; mating begins in January; gestation period 34–37 days; birth March to April; litters of 1–8 young; young above ground at about 6 weeks old.

WHITE-TAILED PRAIRIE DOG

MONTANA

IDAHO

WYOMING

UTAH   COLORADO

RANGE

Approximate normal
range of species.

VITAL STATISTICS

NAME	White-tailed prairie dog *Cynomys leucurus* **SPANISH** perrito de las praderas
DESCRIPTION	Solid, bulky body with short legs and relatively small head, small ears, short tail. Color light brown, buff, or yellowish, may have pinkish tinge; lighter underneath. Patches of darker color present above eyes and on cheeks; nose yellowish. Last half of tail lighter to white. Color may vary due to staining from soil or minerals. Fur short and even in summer, long and rough in winter. Body shape typically sleeker and thinner in winter and spring; fuller to fat in late summer and fall. Males larger than females.
COMPARISON	Only species found in its range. Tail uniform color, unlike black-tailed species.

TOTAL LENGTH	12¼–15 inches (31–38 cm)	TAIL LENGTH	1¼–2½ inches (3.2–6.4 cm)

WEIGHT	24–40 ounces (675–1,125 gm)
TEETH	22 teeth total: incisors 1/1; canines 0/0; premolars 2/1; molars 3/3
HABITAT	Open or slightly brushy ground in high elevation valleys, 5,000–12,000 feet (1,524–3,658 m).
RANGE	Central Rocky Mountains, including western Colorado, eastern Utah, and western Wyoming.
ACTIVITY	Diurnal; may hibernate from late October to March. Sexually mature in 2nd year; mating begins in March; gestation period 28 to 32 days; birth late April to early May; litters of 3–8 young; young above ground at 5–7 weeks old. Less social and with smaller colonies than black-tailed species.

GUNNISON PRAIRIE DOG

RANGE
Approximate normal
range of species.

UTAH   COLORADO

ARIZONA   NEW
MEXICO

VITAL STATISTICS

NAME	**Gunnison prairie dog** *Cynomys gunnisoni* **SPANISH** perrito de las praderas
DESCRIPTION	Solid, bulky body with short legs and relatively small head, short tail. Color buff or yellowish buff with darker hairs intermixed; lighter underneath. Darker areas above eyes and on cheeks. Tail uniform color with tip gray to grayish white. Smallest in body size of all species. Body shape typically sleeker and thinner in winter and spring; fuller to fat in late summer and fall. Males larger than females.
COMPARISON	Only species found in its range. Back darker in color than black-tailed and white-tailed species; tail tipped with gray-colored hair.

TOTAL LENGTH	12–15 inches (30–38 cm)	**TAIL LENGTH**	1½–2½ inches (3.8–6.4 cm)

WEIGHT	23–42 ounces (650–1,190 gm)
TEETH	22 teeth total: incisors 1/1; canines 0/0; premolars 2/1; molars 3/3
HABITAT	Shortgrass prairies located at high elevations, 6,000–12,000 feet (1,829–3,658 m).
RANGE	Southeastern Utah, southwestern Colorado, eastern Arizona, northwestern New Mexico.
ACTIVITY	Diurnal; hibernates in locations where winters are severe. Sexually mature in 2nd year; gestation period of about 30 days; litters average 5 young. Less communal than other species; burrows may lack mounds.

UTAH PRAIRIE DOG

RANGE

Approximate normal range of species.

UTAH

VITAL STATISTICS

NAME	**Utah prairie dog** *Cynomys parvidens* **SPANISH** perrito de las praderas
DESCRIPTION	Solid, bulky body with short legs and relatively small head, small ears, short tail. Color light brown to reddish brown with darker hairs interspersed; lighter underneath. Darker patches above and below eyes. Tail has lighter-colored tip. Body shape typically sleeker and thinner in winter and spring; fuller to fat in late summer and fall. Males larger than females. Classified as a threatened species.
COMPARISON	Only species found in its range.

TOTAL LENGTH	12–14 inches (30–36 cm)	**TAIL LENGTH**	1¼–2½ inches (3.2–6.4 cm)
WEIGHT	24–38 ounces (680–1,080 gm)		
TEETH	22 teeth total: incisors 1/1; canines 0/0; premolars 2/1; molars 3/3		
HABITAT	Shortgrass prairies, from 5,000–9,000 feet (1,524–2,743 m).		
RANGE	South central Utah.		
ACTIVITY	Diurnal; may hibernate during periods of cold weather. Sexually mature in 2nd year; mating begins in early May; gestation period 28 to 32 days; birth late June to early July; litters average 5 young; young above ground at 6 weeks old. Less social and smaller colonies than black-tailed species.		

MEXICAN PRAIRIE DOG

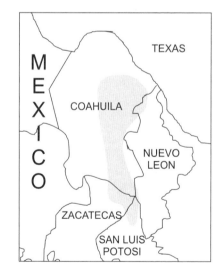

RANGE

Approximate normal range of species.

VITAL STATISTICS

NAME	**Mexican prairie dog** *Cynomys mexicanus* **SPANISH** perrito de las praderas
DESCRIPTION	Solid, bulky body with short legs and relatively small head, short tail. Color tan or beige to brown, may have pinkish tinge; lighter on sides and belly. About half of the tail is darker to black in color, from mid-point to tip. Fur short and even in summer, long and rough in winter. Body shape typically sleeker and thinner in winter and spring; fuller to fat in late summer and fall. Males larger than females. Classified as an endangered species.
COMPARISON	Only species found in its range. Has black-tipped tail similar to black-tailed species, but is smaller in body size.

TOTAL LENGTH	15–17 inches (38–43 cm)	**TAIL LENGTH**	2½–4 inches (6–10 cm)

WEIGHT	32–42 ounces (907–1,191 gm)
TEETH	22 teeth total: incisors 1/1; canines 0/0; premolars 2/1; molars 3/3
HABITAT	Open plains and plateaus in intermontane basins with gypsum and xerosol soils; elevations from 5,250–7,200 feet (1,600–2,195 m).
RANGE	Northeastern Mexico in southern Coahuila and San Luis Potosi.
ACTIVITY	Diurnal; active throughout year. Sexually mature in 2nd year; mating begins in early January; gestation period about 1 month; litters average 4 young.

MISTAKEN IDENTITY:
THE ROCK SQUIRREL

A species similar to prairie dogs is the rock squirrel, one of many kinds of ground squirrels. Rock squirrels (*Citellus variegatus*) live throughout southwestern North America, from northern Utah and Colorado southward into central Mexico. Rock squirrels are smaller than prairie dogs, averaging about 10–11 inches long (25.4–28 cm), and have tails that are distinctly longer than prairie dogs, almost as long as their bodies. Body color ranges from gray to brown. Rock squirrels rarely live in the open prairie, but prefer rocky slopes and canyons. Unlike prairie dogs, rock squirrels do not live in colonies, but are solitary. They do, however, make the same kind of yelping bark as prairie dogs and live underground in burrows. If there are no other similar animals in sight and there is a tail as long as the body, what you are seeing is most likely a rock squirrel, not a prairie dog.

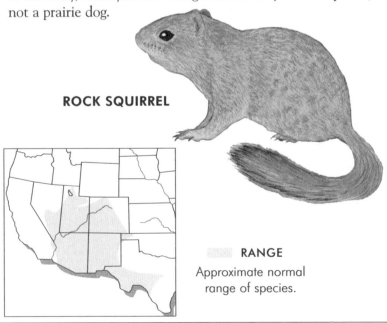

ROCK SQUIRREL

RANGE

Approximate normal range of species.

EVOLUTION

"It rather appears to occupy a middle ground betwixt the rabbit and squirrel — like the former in feeding and burrowing — like the latter in frisking, flirting, sitting erect, and somewhat so in its barking."

— Josiah Gregg (1845, *Commerce of the Prairies*)

Rodents go far back in evolutionary history, emerging as a distinct group of mammals during the late Paleocene Epoch, about fifty-five million years ago. Among rodents, the closest relatives of prairie dogs are ground squirrels, specifically the genus *Spermophilus*, which includes species such as the rock squirrel, the thirteen-lined rock squirrel, and the golden-mantled ground squirrel.

Prairie dogs and ground squirrels diverged from a common ancestry between two and three million years ago. Since then, physical differences between them have primarily involved teeth pattern, but prairie dogs have also gradually developed a distinctive lifestyle that involves closely knit cooperative groups, something missing with ground squirrel populations. One theory regarding this diversion proposes that modern prairie dogs first appeared as a genetic variation out of a population of early ground squirrels somewhere in the southern part of the Rocky Mountains, most likely during the Pliocene era.

As this new variation spread in numbers, populations that inhabited different kinds of terrain gradually adapted to become more efficient at surviving in their local conditions and in the process, promoted the development of the five modern species. The greatest influence was the Rocky Mountains themselves, a major physical barrier that isolated species on the western side, while encouraging faster development for those on the east, where the wide open plains and changing environmental conditions triggered changes.

Fossils of early prairie dogs and their ancestors have been discovered in parts of the range they now inhabit, mostly limited to the

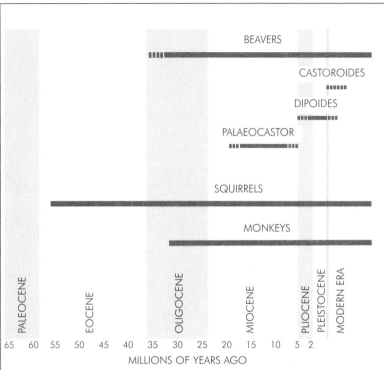

BEAVERS

CASTOROIDES

DIPOIDES

PALAEOCASTOR

SQUIRRELS

MONKEYS

| PALEOCENE | EOCENE | OLIGOCENE | MIOCENE | PLIOCENE | PLEISTOCENE | MODERN ERA |

65   60   55   50   45   40   35   30   25   20   15   10   5   2

MILLIONS OF YEARS AGO

Different animals evolved during different geologic eras but evidence about the origin of rodents is more complex and doubtful than for most other kinds of mammals. Based on existing fossil records, prairie dogs probably began to emerge as a distinct order early in the Oligocene, which began about 37 million years ago.

territory of the black-tailed prairie dog. One of these earlier animal forms is called *Cynomus spispiza*, found in what is now South Dakota. This creature had features similar to both the modern black-tailed prairie dog and the white-tailed prairie dog. Another early example is *Cynomus meadensis*, found in Kansas. This animal dates to the early Pleistocene and was smaller than the modern black-tailed prairie dog. In general, the fossil record of early prairie dogs indicates that the older the species, the smaller the animal.

The earliest fossil found that is similar to modern prairie dogs comes from Kansas and has been dated to what is called the Kansas glacial period of the Pleistocene. Some earlier forms of prairie dogs may have coexisted with modern forms and then died out. But in the Great Plains, paleontologists have not found any record of these early prairie dogs by the time of the Wisconsin glacial period, when modern prairie dogs prevailed.

Among the five species of prairie dogs now recognized, the black-tailed and the Mexican prairie dogs are thought to have changed the most when compared to their ancient relatives, the ground squirrels. The Gunnison prairie dog, on the other hand, represents a slightly more primitive form.

These comparisons, which traditionally relied on minor details in skeleton structure and teeth, are now increasingly reliant on variations in gene structure. Based on such genetic evidence, the two other prairie dog species, the white-tailed and the Utah varieties, appear to scientists to be closer in structure to the Gunnison prairie dog than to the black-tailed species.

On the other hand, there is a very close relationship between the black-tailed species and the Mexican prairie dog. It has been suggested that they could be considered minor variations on the same species, with the Mexican prairie dog once part of the same wide-ranging population of black-tails before climactic changes created a massive barrier between north and south—the Sonoran and Chihuahuan deserts.

TAXONOMY

"The funny, frisky little prairie dog — a condensed or foreshortened gray squirrel — barks with amusing alarm at your approach, then drops into his hole, which, for mutual defense and advantage, he shares with an owl and a rattlesnake, and is silent as the grave till you pass out of hearing."
— Horace Greeley (1869, essay in *Harper's Magazine*)

In the science of species classification, taxonomists work to understand the relationship among plants and animals by defining their differences. Following this scheme, prairie dogs are classified as members of the rodent order, one of twenty-seven living orders of mammals and the largest group of mammals. Among rodents, twenty-eight families and more than two thousand different species are now recognized.

The Muridae family, representing most kinds of rats, mice, and voles, has 1,336 species and the Sciuridae, representing squirrels, chipmunks, and marmots in addition to prairie dogs, has 272 species. Prairie dogs are only found in North America and are represented by two subgenera that differ little in appearance, *Cynomys* Rafinesque and *Leucocrossuromys* Hollister. Between these two categories, there are five species currently recognized.

The black-tailed prairie dog (*Cynomys ludovicianus*) is the most widespread of all prairie dog species and is a member of subgenus *Cynomys* Rafinesque. The Mexican prairie dog (*Cynomys mexicanus*) also fits within this group. Within the subgenus *Leucocrossuromys* Hollister are the remaining three species, the white-tailed prairie dog (*Cynomys leucurus*), the Utah prairie dog (*Cynomys parvidens*), and the Gunnison prairie dog (*Cynomys gunnisoni*).

Some taxonomists also support a further subdivision of these species. For black-tailed prairie dogs, two subspecies are recognized, the plains variety (*Cynomys ludovicianus ludovicianus*) — those inhabiting territory to the east of the Rocky Mountains, and the

SCIENTIFIC CLASSIFICATION

KINGDOM	• Animals
PHYLUM	• Chordata (vertebrates)
CLASS	• Mammalia (mammals)
ORDER	• Rodentia (rodents)
FAMILY	• Sciuridae
SUBFAMILY	• Sciuridae
TRIBE	• Marmotini
SUBTRIBE	• Spermophilina (ground squirrels, prairie dogs)
SUBGENUS	• *Cynomys Rafinesque*
GENUS	• *Cynomys*
SPECIES	• *ludovicianus*

Arizona variety, (*Cynomys ludovicianus arizonensis*) — found in Arizona, southern New Mexico, western Texas, and northern Mexico. The differences between the two subspecies are insignificant and their physical appearance is identical, even to trained observers.

One of the main characteristics that classifies prairie dogs as rodents is the two matching pair of incisors at the front of their jaws, which are specialized teeth that keep growing throughout the life of the animal. All rodents share this characteristic. Another defining feature of rodent teeth is a gap between the incisors in front and the teeth on the side — the site on the jaw where canine and premolar teeth are found in other mammal orders.

The bone structure of rodent skulls is also unique, having developed to provide appropriate anchor points for the oversized muscles that go along with rodent jaws, allowing them to make better use of

WORLD MAMMALS

ORDER	DESCRIPTION	No. of FAMILIES	No. of SPECIES
MONOTREMES	spiny anteaters, echidna	2	3
DIDELPHIMORPHIA	American opossums	4	66
PAUCITUBERCULATA	shrew opossums	1	7
MICROBIOTHERIA	monito del monte	1	1
DASYUROMORPHIA	carnivorous marsupials	3	64
PERAMELEMORPHIA	bandicoots	2	22
NOTORYCTEMORPHIA	marsupial mole	1	1
DIPROTODONTIA	koala, wombats, kangaroos	10	131
XENARTHRA	sloths, anteaters, armadillos	4	29
INSECTIVORA	hedgehogs, moles, shrews	7	440
SCANDENTIA	tree shrews	1	16
DERMOPTERA	flying lemurs	1	2
CHIROPTERA	bats	18	977
PRIMATES	monkeys, apes, lemurs	15	279
CARNIVORA	dogs, cats, bears, weasels	8	246
PINNIPEDIA	seals, walruses, sea lions	3	34
CETACEA	whales, dolphins, porpoises	13	78
SIRENIA	sea cows, manatees, dugongs	2	4
PROBOSCIDEA	elephants	1	2
PERISSODACTYLA	horses, tapirs, rhinos	3	17
HYRACOIDEA	hyraxes	1	7
TUBULIDENTATA	aardvark	1	1
ARTIODACTYLA	pigs, hippos, giraffes, deer	10	221
PHOLIDOTA	pangolins	1	7
RODENTIA	rats, squirrels, prairie dogs	28	2,047
LAGOMORPHA	rabbits, hares, pikas	2	81
MACROSCELIDEA	elephant shrews	1	15

The classification shown here is from *Walker's Mammals of the World, Sixth Edition.* (1999, Johns Hopkins University Press)

their incisors as gnawing tools. Other defining characteristics of rodents include two distinct bones in their lower arms, fur covering most of the body, and extended tails in a variety of forms.

The general structure of the skull and the design of the teeth not only differentiate rodents from other mammals, they are also used to organize rodents into two suborders, the Sciurognathi and the Hystricognathi. Prairie dogs are grouped into the former, along with beavers, squirrels, rats, and pocket gophers; the latter includes porcupines, guinea pigs, and capybaras.

The range in body size among rodents is tremendous. The smallest is the pygmy mouse, barely two inches in length (5 cm), found in the southwestern United States south through central Mexico to Central America. The largest is the capybara, four feet long (1.2 m), a resident of South America and found in Panama, Colombia, and south to Argentina. Next to capybaras, beavers are the second largest of all rodents and are the largest rodents on the North American continent. Marmots are slightly smaller than beavers and prairie dogs are smaller yet, but they are still relatively large compared to tree squirrels, mice, and other North American rodents.

Although taxonomists generally agree on what makes a specific kind of animal a certain species, they do not always agree on how to group species into families or suborders. With rodents, some taxonomists believe that instead of two suborders, there should be three. In past scientific eras, such distinctions were the basis of detailed ongoing research and discussion, basing the final organization on details of skeletal structure.

In the newest scientific era, now under way, taxonomists are increasingly turning to DNA analysis to establish links between species as well as crucial differences. The genetic material in guinea pigs, for example, has been shown to be closer to that of rabbits, horses, and primates than to that of other rodents, but these native South American animals have not been reclassified because of this evidence, and may never be. Prairie dogs, on the other hand, appear well-established as distinct members of the rodent order, and their traditional taxonomic place is as yet unchallenged.

WORLD RODENTS

AFRICAN BUSH SQUIRREL

SPRINGHARE

GIANT FLYING SQUIRREL

POCKET GOPHER

PATAGONIAN CAVY

KANGAROO RAT

WORLD RODENTS

FAMILY	DESCRIPTION	No. of GENERA	No. of SPECIES
APLODONTIDAE	mountain beaver	1	1
SCIURIDAE	prairie dogs, squirrels, chipmunks, marmots	51	272
CASTORIDAE	beavers	1	2
GEOMYIDAE	pocket gophers	6	40
HETEROMYIDAE	pocket mice, kangaroo rats	6	60
DIPODIDAE	jumping mice, jerboas	17	51
MURIDAE	old world rats, voles, mice	301	1,336
ANOMALURIDAE	scaly-tailed squirrels	3	7
PEDETIDAE	springhaas	1	1
CTENODACTYLIDAE	gundis	4	5
MYOXIDAE	dormice	10	28
BATHYERGIDAE	African mole rats	5	14
HYSTRICIDAE	old world porcupines	3	11
PETROMURIDAE	dassie rat	1	1
THRYONOMYIDAE	cane rats	1	2
ERETHIZONTIDAE	new world porcupines	4	12
CHINCHILLIDAE	chinchillas, viscachas	3	6
DINOMYIDAE	pacarana	1	1
CAVIIDAE	cavies, guinea pigs, maras	5	17
HYDROCHOERIDAE	capybaras	1	1
DASYPROCTIDAE	agoutis	2	13
AGOUTIDAE	pacas	1	2
CTENOMYIDAE	tuco-tucos	1	48
OCTODONTIDAE	octodonts, degus	6	11
ABROCOMIDAE	chinchilla rats	1	5
ECHIMYIDAE	spiny rats, rock rats	19	73
CAPROMYIDAE	hutias	8	26
MYOCASTORIDAE	nutria	1	1

The classification shown here is from *Walker's Mammals of the World, Sixth Edition.* (1999, Johns Hopkins University Press)

RANGE

"No animals in these western regions interested me so much as the prairie dogs. These lively little fellows select for the site of their towns a level piece of prairie with a sandy or gravelly soil, out of which they can excavate their dwellings with great facility. Being of a merry, sociable disposition, they, unlike the bear or wolf, choose to live in a large community, where laws exist for the public good, and there is less danger to be apprehended from the attacks of their numerous and crafty enemies."

— George Frederick Ruxton (1916, *Wild Life in the Rocky Mountains*)

Long before settlers began migrating into the western states in the 1800s, prairie dogs were one of the most visible mammals on the plains. Traditional prairie dog territory begins just west of the Missouri River, a range that covers most of what are now thirteen western states: Arizona, Colorado, Idaho, Kansas, Montana, Nebraska, New Mexico, North Dakota, Oklahoma, South Dakota, Texas, Utah, and Wyoming. Portions of the original range also extended north into Canada, covering thousands of square miles in southern Alberta and Saskatchewan, and south into Mexico, into the states of Chihuahua and Sonora.

Estimates of the territory originally inhabited by these social rodents vary, but are in the range of hundreds of million of acres. At least 200 million acres were occupied by the black-tailed prairie dog alone and at the extreme, their colonies may have covered up to 700 million acres. The original range is estimated to have taken up to 20 percent of the total spread of short- and mixed-grass prairies.

Although some prairie dog colonies could be extremely large, stretching over hundreds of acres, most were smaller. Individual colonies were scattered throughout the landscape, typically located where there was a deep layer of soil and the ground was relatively flat and treeless.

Together, the original range of the five prairie dog species covered much of the Great Plains from Canada to Mexico, as well as large areas west of the Rocky Mountains. This area matched the original extent of short- and mid-grass prairies, the preferred habitat for prairie dogs. Scattered groups of prairie dogs can still be found throughout this expanse, but only a few percent of their original numbers are left.

All five species of prairie dogs occupy separate ranges, with no part of their natural ranges overlapping. The largest of these is occupied by black-tailed prairie dogs, extending into Canada in the north and Mexico in the south, and approximately between the Rocky Mountains in the west and the Missouri River in the east.

PRAIRIE DOG RANGE

ARIZONA

The original range of black-tailed prairie dogs covered an estimated 650,000 acres in the southeast; the last colony, located near Apache, disappeared about 1960.

COLORADO

As much as 7 million acres were originally occupied by prairie dog east of the Rocky Mountains; the land here was heavily populated with colonies. Current estimates put the remaining range at 44,000 to 90,000 acres.

IDAHO

Colonies of white-tailed prairie dogs extended into the southeastern corner of the state. The original size of the range and estimated numbers are unknown.

KANSAS

The original range of black-tailed prairie dogs was an estimated 2 to 2.5 million acres, about 5 percent of the land in the state. This has dropped by almost 99 percent, to less than 40,000 acres.

MONTANA

Colonies originally covered about 1.5 million acres; by the 1990s, the population had dropped by about 95 percent and now occupies less than 70,000 acres.

NEBRASKA

This state represents one of the largest original prairie dog territories, with an estimated 6 million acres of land occupied by colonies. By the 1990s, this area had shrunk by 99 percent, to about 60,000 acres.

NEW MEXICO

About 12 million acres were originally covered with prairie dog colonies; recent studies report that their current range is only about 15,000 acres, a reduction of 99.9 percent.

NORTH DAKOTA

Prairie dogs once occupied up to 2 million acres throughout the state; currently, about 15,000 acres are occupied, confined to only seven counties.

STATE-BY-STATE

OKLAHOMA

Much of the land in the western part of the state was originally occupied; colonies covered at least several million acres. By the 1990s, this territory had shrunk to less than 10,000 acres, all confined to the panhandle area of the state.

SOUTH DAKOTA

Traditionally home to as much as 1.8 million acres of prairie dog colonies, about 240,000 acres of this territory is now occupied.

TEXAS

Up to 57 million acres of land were originally occupied by prairie dog colonies; the latest estimates report that this territory has shrunk to about 23,000 acres. The original range was concentrated in the northwest section of the state.

UTAH

The Utah prairie dog is found in the central part of the state; Gunnison prairie dog range is limited to the extreme southeastern part of the state. The white-tailed prairie dog range is in the northeast area and is thought to be about 60–65 percent of its original size.

WYOMING

Here, prairie dog colonies may have once extended up to 16 million acres. At latest count, the size of their range is thought to be less than 200,000 acres.

CANADA

Canada is currently home to black-tailed prairie dogs only in extreme southern Saskatchewan, part of their original range, which covered the southeastern section of Alberta as well.

MEXICO

Prairie dog territory originally extended over about 1.4 million acres, including territory in Chihuahua, Sonora, Cohuila, Nuevo Leon, Zacatecas, and San Luis Potosi. In Chihuahua, the latest estimate is about 90,000 acres; the remaining range includes areas of Coahuila and Nuevo Leon.

This range probably fluctuated over time, condensing and expanding from the effects of weather conditions — especially floods and droughts — climate changes, and disease. With the arrival of large numbers of settlers from the eastern states, however, new forces made an impact on prairie dog towns. In some cases, the introduction of open range grazing for cattle triggered expansion of existing prairie dog populations, because in some areas the cattle removed native vegetation that was too tall for the fussy demands of prairie dogs. They typically avoid vegetation that is tall enough to conceal predators and even though they are able to keep a limited amount of grasses nibbled low to the ground, they avoid habitats where vegetation exceeds their gnawing abilities.

Ranching and farming also destroyed predators that helped keep prairie dog populations in check, triggering faster population growth

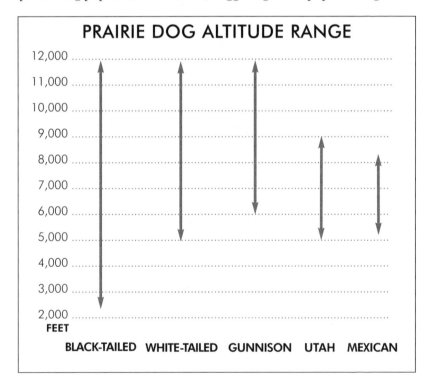

PRAIRIE DOG ALTITUDE RANGE

in colonies. At the same time, however, both ranchers and farmers generally found prairie dogs a nuisance. Their burrows were considered a danger to horses and cattle and their appetites a threat to crops. In addition, the location of colonies in some areas was also coveted for homes, roads, and towns. These forces working against prairie dogs are still a major issue in parts of their remaining range in the present.

By the early 1900s, organized efforts to eradicate prairie dogs were common throughout the West, with local, state, and national governments supporting eradication activities. The results were spectacular, with entire prairie dog colonies destroyed in weeks or months. By the end of the 1900s, the original range of prairie dogs had been reduced to less than 700,000 acres, and in most areas, this range is still shrinking. The accidental introduction of the plague on the West Coast in the late 1800s also provided a deadly natural weapon, wiping out entire colonies in days as it spread to the east.

BIOLOGY

"They are close-haired, even to the tail; the cheek-pouches are small; the nail of the thumb is well developed; and the forepaws with their crooked claws, are very effective instruments for the mining operations in which the lusty and truculent little creatures engage so extensively."

— *The Riverside Natural History* (1884)

TEETH

All rodents are characterized by two sets of prominent incisors in the front of their jaws, one set in the upper jaw and one in the lower. These sharp teeth grow continuously throughout an animal's life; constant chewing keeps the growth in check by wearing down the cutting surface. Incisors consist of two layers, a hard front enamel that forms the actual cutting edge and a softer material behind.

The softer material is constantly abraded away by the action of gnawing. Like other rodents, prairie dogs keep their incisors in use — and sharp — mostly through grazing, but they may also occasionally gnaw on inedible objects. Also, these animals may gnash their incisors together at times as a form of threat display to other prairie dogs, perhaps helping to hone the cutting surface further.

Although most of the prairie dog diet is relatively soft plant tissue — the leaves and stems of grasses — the incisors can be used to chew through much tougher material, including brush, small tree limbs, and heavy underground roots. Prairie dogs have also been known to burrow through soft rock, using both their heavy, hardened claws and their teeth. Once plant material has been detached, matching sets of molars are used to grind it into smaller pieces, preparing it for the digestive system.

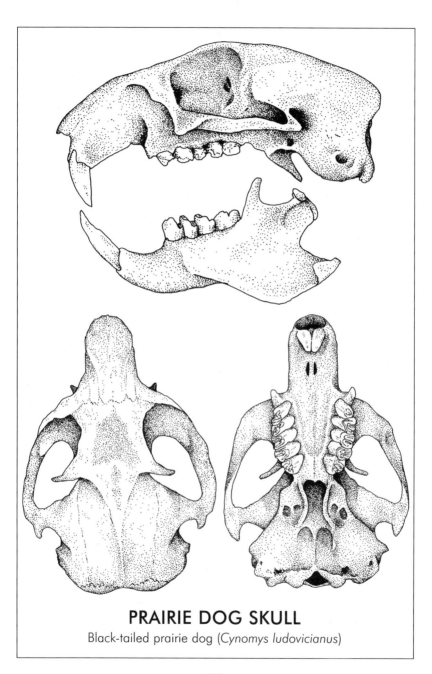

PRAIRIE DOG SKULL
Black-tailed prairie dog (*Cynomys ludovicianus*)

EYESIGHT

Prairie dogs rely on eyesight to survive. They must be able to identify threats — predators such as raptors or coyotes — in advance, giving them enough time to escape to the relative safety of their burrows. Compared to the overall size of the head, the eyes are moderately large. And the construction of the prairie dog visual system is particularly well suited to the scanning it must do.

The visual system has the ability to perceive and focus on objects well above the center of the eye — a useful feature when there are predators on the wing — and the retina is thought to be especially sensitive, producing sharp and detailed images. Eyesight in prairie dogs has evolved to perform best in daylight hours. They are active only during the day when they come above ground to feed. At night or underground, they do not have the ability to see very well. When underground, they rely on other senses, especially smell and touch, to navigate and perform other activities.

Despite their acute eyesight, prairie dogs suffer from poor depth perception; tame animals have been known to walk off the edge of tables, being unable to sense the danger of height. Prairie dogs, as well as squirrels, are also color blind in the red/green spectrum and can only see blues, yellows, and grays.

TAIL

Prairie dog tails are relatively short — only several inches long on average — and rarely equal one fourth the length of their body. The tail functions mostly for communication with other prairie dogs, signalling aggression, friendliness, alertness, or alarm. It is also helpful for identification; in the black-tailed species, the tip of the tail in adults is brown to dark brown in color, darker than the rest of the tail or body.

FEET

Short, stubby legs limit the mobility of prairie dogs. They are not fast runners and they are unable to jump more than a few inches. Yet these limbs are ideally suited for the lifestyle of the animal —

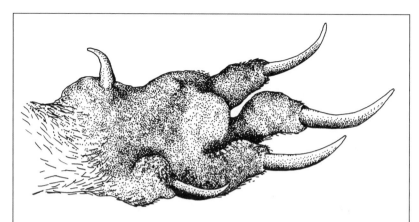

The underside of the front paw of the prairie dog is covered with a tough layer of skin, a necessary characteristic for animals that do a lot of digging.

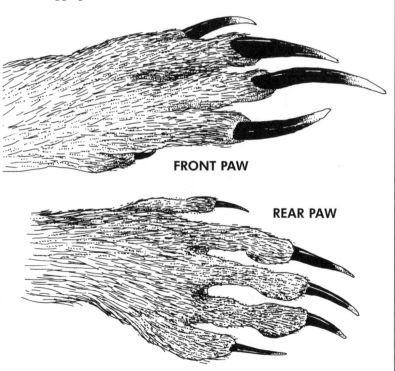

FRONT PAW

REAR PAW

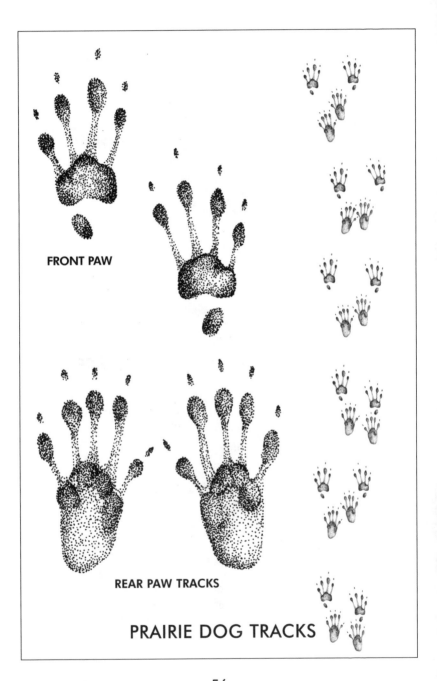

FRONT PAW

REAR PAW TRACKS

PRAIRIE DOG TRACKS

the right shape and size for digging burrows in the ground and giving them the right kind of locomotion through these burrows.

Claws are what really turn their legs into useful tools. Each paw has five claws, with the claws on the forelegs larger than those on the back. Tough and dense, the claws have developed the necessary strength to give prairie dogs an edge useful for their safety. Though not often used in self-defense, claws are efficient in loosening and removing soil in the construction of their burrows.

HAIR

Prairie dogs are covered with a mostly uniform coat of fur, which is thicker in the winter and sparser in the summer. The hair in the winter coat is also usually longer and slightly darker in color. The individual hairs that make up the coat are flat in shape, darker at the base, and often black or darker at the tip. Darker strands are mixed with these hairs, combining to give a grizzled appearance.

Prairie dogs tend to look pretty much alike in terms of fur color, with relatively little variation from light to dark. But like most groups of mammals, two distinct extremes also can occur. In albino individuals, where the fur is lacking pigment the color is white or

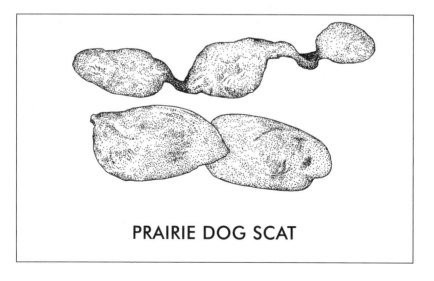

PRAIRIE DOG SCAT

very pale. In melanistic individuals the fur has more than the usual pigment, resulting in color that is black, dark brown, or very dark in general.

Because all prairie dogs spend a lot of time underground in narrow burrows surrounded by soil, their hair can become discolored by pigments in the dirt, making it darker or altering the color in other ways. In some parts of their range, for example, prairie dogs may have orange or reddish streaks or tints to their coats, the result of iron oxides in the soil or black tints from coal deposits.

Many mammals have a regular pattern of hair replacement, a cycle referred to as molting. With prairie dogs, fur is shed and replaced twice a year and occasionally more. The major reason for this activity is to replace heavier, denser fur — grown to provide protection in the winter months — with a coat more suitable to the hot weather of the summer, and vice versa. Molting occurs in a general pattern, beginning in spring with the fur on the belly and underparts of an animal. The pattern progresses to the sides, beginning around the head and moving to the rear. In the fall, the pattern is the opposite, with replacement beginning near the tail and working its way to the front; the belly is last. Molting in black-tailed prairie dogs occurs over a period of one to two weeks, but can vary according to altitude and how far north the animals are located. Weather patterns can also affect when molting occurs and how long it takes. In general, the cycle can vary from year to year, occurring one to two months later in some cases.

Baby prairie dogs are born hairless, but acquire their first coat of fur within two to three weeks after birth. Their first molt is at the end of their first summer.

REPRODUCTION

*"This noisy spermophile, or marmot, is found in numbers,
sometimes hundreds of families together, living in burrows
on the prairies; and their galleries are so extensive as to
render riding among them quite unsafe in many places."*
— Reverend John Bachman (1851, *Audubon's Mammals*)

The breeding season for prairie dogs is in the winter, usually from late January to March. This time frame varies depending on local weather conditions, the immediate availability of food, and how much food was available the previous year. In northern parts of their range, the breeding season is usually delayed, beginning in March or April; in the warmer, southern regions, breeding can begin as early as January. During this period, mating almost always takes place underground and males may mate with females multiple times.

Females typically begin breeding during their second year. They enter estrus, or breeding condition, for two to three weeks, during which time they mate with males and are able to get pregnant. One exception is the Gunnison prairie dog, in which estrus lasts for only one day.

Among the black-tailed prairie dog, more than 80 percent of the females will only mate with the dominant resident male of their coterie; Gunnison's females, on the other hand, exhibit this preference only 35 percent of the time. Most black-tailed females are also monogamous, mating with only one male during a breeding cycle.

Prairie dogs may alter their breeding preferences, switching from monogamy to multiple mates as conditions in habitat change, such as greater or lesser supplies of food. Such a shift might be a survival tactic, helping expand the mix of genes in a local population. It might also just be a consequence of what happens when animals change their feeding behavior in response to the amount of food available; the more area covered in order to find food, the more

YOUNG PRAIRIE DOG,
ONE-DAY OLD

YOUNG PRAIRIE DOG,
THREE-DAYS OLD

YOUNG PRAIRIE DOG, THIRTY-THREE DAYS OLD

likely neighboring animals will come in contact with each other.

Although mating takes place underground and out of sight of observers, the males in some species exhibit a unique above ground behavior after mating. These males emerge from their burrows and give a special mating call, from two to twenty-five barks produced in one or more sets. Some males of the Gunnison's species will also dust bathe after copulation. Males of the black-tailed species sometimes perform a different breeding-related behavior, actively carrying nesting material into burrows just before mating.

Prairie dogs only mate once a year, but in some circumstances, females may go into heat a second time, probably due to initial breeding activity that does not result in pregnancy. This has been observed in both black-tailed and Gunnison prairie dogs.

The gestation period in female prairie dogs lasts about a month, from twenty-eight to thirty-two days. Average size of a litter is four, but females may give birth to as few as one or as many as eight babies. When the pups are born, they are about 2½–2¾ inches (65 to 70 mm) long and weigh about half an ounce (16 gm). The pups are born without hair and with their eyes closed.

Like most rodents, young prairie dogs grow rapidly. By the second or third week after birth, they begin to acquire their first coat of fur, which is thin and light. Their eyes open about four to five weeks after birth. Young prairie dogs remain underground for at least the first six weeks, attended constantly by one or more female members of the family group. At about seven to eight weeks of age, they are weaned and begin eating for themselves. Young prairie dogs continue growing until they are about one and a half years old.

One unusual aspect of prairie dog family life is the occurrence of infanticide, the killing of pups while they are still young. In most cases, pups are killed by a female family member living in the same coterie, a relative of the pups' mother. And in some cases, the young are not only killed, but partially consumed by the killer. Infanticide also occurs when prairie dogs from neighboring coteries invade a family burrow, and occasionally when the pups have been abandoned by their mother. In one study of black-tailed prairie dogs in South Dakota, infanticide was found to be the greatest cause of death in young pups, generating mortality in up to half of all litters born.

ACTIVITY

"In their habits they are clannish, social, and extremely convivial, never living alone like other animals, but, on the contrary, always found in villages or large settlements. They are a wild, frolicsome, madcap set of fellows when undisturbed, uneasy and ever on the move, and appear to take special delight in chattering away the time, and visiting from hole to hole to gossip and talk over each other's affairs."

— G. Wilkins Kendall (1844, *Across the Great Southwestern Prairies*)

Adult prairie dogs seem to spend most of their time above ground during daylight hours. Some observers say this may be as much as 95 percent of all daylight hours during most of the year. Others have noted that one third to one fourth of daylight hours are spent inside burrows. Some above ground activity includes greeting family members and neighbors, scanning for predators, and resting. Depending on how many predators there may be in a specific area, prairie dogs spend from 40 to 50 percent of their time on the alert and actively searching for threats, with the remainder of the time topside spent eating, sunning, or playing.

Prairie dogs are not built to be swift runners. Most of their defense consists of sticking close to their burrows and relying on observation — especially that of others in the colony — to give them an advance warning of danger. Once an alarm is sounded — the barking call that is most characteristic of this animal — a prairie dog will rush to the nearest burrow entrance. If further consideration of a threat is needed, it will pause on top of an entrance mound and make alarm calls while assessing the situation. If the danger increases, the animal will enter its burrow, but often only to stick its head out, continuing to bark and assess. Still more danger and it will back farther down the burrow.

In some colonies, the pattern of vegetation may entice individuals to wander far from their burrows, but in most sites, adults rarely venture more than a hundred feet or so from this refuge.

During the hottest times of the year, prairie dogs still spend a lot of time above ground in order to feed, but they make periodical visits underground. Most likely, this is to seek the cooling shelter found there. In various parts of their range, the underground breaks may last from fifteen to twenty minutes or up to a few hours.

During the winter, cold weather or storms may keep the animals underground for longer periods, up to several days or more. Although inactive during this time, the most common species, the black-tailed prairie dog, does not hibernate. In other species, however, hibernation is a biological response to the shortened hours of daylight and the appearance of cold temperatures. This is particularly true of the white-tailed prairie dog, which hibernates from October to March at the extreme. Gunnison prairie dogs and the Utah species also hibernate. The Mexican prairie dog, similar to the black-tailed species, does not.

While underground, all species of prairie dogs spend time digging new burrows, repairing damage to existing burrows, and removing loose soil and other debris that builds up from use. Burrows are also the preferred site for mating and nursing.

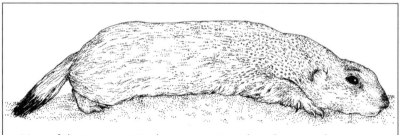

Most of the time, prairie dogs are active when they are above ground, with the majority of their time here spent eating and watching out for predators. But they may also occasionally spend time basking in the sun.

One of the most effective postures for watching out for predators is sitting upright, allowing them to see farther away from their burrows.

When a predator is sighted, prairie dogs may respond in different ways, depending on how far away the danger lies and the relative threat associated with a particular animal. At the highest alert level, a vigilant prairie dog will stand upright, allowing the most unobstructed view.

As a potentially dangerous animal approaches, a prairie dog will respond with a sequence of reactions. Already close to the safety of their burrow, the first stage is a crouch, ready to make a dash for the burrow entrance.

Depending on how fast the danger is approaching, the prairie dog will constantly reassess the danger, moving closer to the burrow when necessary.

The entrance to the burrow provides a safe vantage point from which to make a final decision about a predator. Ultimately, when the predator comes close enough, the prairie dog will drop completely into the burrow, but still remain a few feet below the surface, waiting to see if further retreat is necessary.

Mutual grooming is a major social activity practiced by these animals. Using their incisors, two or more prairie dogs comb through each others' fur, an activity that not only promotes bonding between animals but is helpful in removing dirt and parasites. Another mutual activity performed above ground is play, most often by pups and younger animals. Because underground observation reports are scarce, it is possible that prairie dogs may do all of these things in their burrows as well.

In family burrows, prairie dogs often sleep in groups. The typical sleeping posture consists of a hunched-over sitting position, with the forelegs crossed and the head slumped down into the back legs. Alternately, prairie dogs will lie on their backs with their feet in the air, sometimes resting their heads on the bodies of others. The sleeping site is usually a chamber, dug out as a side room from a burrow pathway.

Weather conditions can affect the time spent above ground. Rain or snow generally keeps animals underground, but wind or extreme heat are rarely enough to keep them from coming up to feed,

Mutual grooming is frequently practiced by prairie dogs. This activity helps strengthen bonds between individuals and family members, but it also performs a useful function, keeping fur clean and helping control parasites.

although high heat will limit the amount of time they spend away from the protective coolness of their burrows.

Prairie dog species that do not hibernate will venture above ground when snow is present. They root through snow searching for sources of food, burrowing up through it when it is sufficiently thick to cover the entrances to their burrows. Some animals are also willing to stay out in the rain to feed, as long as the rainfall is not too intense.

Although they are social animals, prairie dogs can be aggressive when it comes to defending their territory. Their biggest threat comes from neighbors searching for food and males searching for females (during the breeding season). Aggressive displays and charges are the most usual reactions to such threats, but these normally docile creatures have been observed nipping and clawing interloping neighbors, sometimes causing injuries.

Dominant males are most likely to defend territory, rising earlier and being more alert than others in a colony. But adult females will also participate, particularly when there are pups in residence.

HIBERNATION

"It has been supposed that the prairie-dog hibernates; but this is not the case, though he lays in a store of provision for winter consumption — he being as lively at that period as at any other, though he wisely prefers keeping within the house while the icy blasts blow across the plains."

— William H.G. Kingston (1884, *The Western World*)

Hibernation is a biological response to seasonal conditions, particularly the length of daylight hours and temperature. During hibernation, an animal's metabolism slows. It takes fewer breaths and the number of heartbeats per minute is reduced. The result is less need for its body to burn energy, thereby allowing it to go for longer stretches without eating.

Some species of prairie dogs hibernate and others do not. Hibernators include the Gunnison prairie dog, the Utah prairie dog, and the white-tailed prairie dog. Black-tailed prairie dogs and Mexican prairie dogs do not hibernate.

Depending on altitude and latitude, hibernation may begin as early as late fall, but typically begins during winter. White-tailed prairie dogs exhibit the longest hibernation, often entering this state in October and not becoming active again until March or April of the following spring.

Although black-tailed and Mexican prairie dogs are not hibernators, they may spend as much as several weeks underground during cold weather. This response to the weather conditions typically involves very little activity and can resemble hibernation, but the biological response is different.

COMMUNICATION

"Their sharp cries are incessant; as each note is emitted the body shakes and the tail jerks, the whole appearance being ludicrously like a toy barking-dog, which squeaks and drops the jaw as you press the little bellows."

— *The Riverside Natural History* (1884)

Prairie dogs have developed a rich and varied menu of calls used for communication with their family members and neighbors. Their name, in fact, stems from their signature "bark," a yipping sound that reminded early western explorers of domesticated dogs.

Much of the sound that visitors hear from a prairie dog colony are variations of alarm calls, from single barks to two-note barks, usually accompanied by the up-and-down flicking of the tail. Serious threats are marked by the most urgent calls, often emitted with the calling animal standing on its hind legs and thrusting its head upward as it utters its calls. Although they may look like inconsequential mammals, prairie dogs not only make sophisticated judgments about the severity of an intruder or threat, they can even identify individual animals, including humans.

In one study, black-tailed prairie dogs gradually became accustomed to the presence of humans over months and years of close observation. Detailed examination of voice prints made of their calls while human observers were present indicated they altered their alarm calls consistently, matching specific calls to individuals, even when those people wore different clothes.

Even more specifically, subtle variations in calls would indicate a change in the color of a person's clothes; whether a person was tall or short; how fast a person was moving; and whether a person was carrying a gun. The systematic analysis of calls also showed that some or this information was remembered for periods of up to two months.

Other studies of prairie dog calls show that individual colonies

Prairie dogs make alarm calls from a variety of postures, including sitting and standing. The posture can be linked to the degree of threat, with the most danger involving a more upright position, the better to be heard by other prairie dogs in the area.

have distinctive dialects even though the alarm calls, representing the basic language, remain the same. That is, a colony from one area will make calls that differ from those in another area, just as people from northeastern cities pronounce some words different than do people from southern cities. And just as geographic distance can make these dialect differences more pronounced in humans, studies have shown that the farther apart prairie dog colonies are, the more pronounced the difference can be in their calls. The differences may also be compounded by separation from other colonies due to significant geographical barriers such as deserts or by altitudes.

More than ten different types of calls are used by prairie dogs to communicate. These range from a variety of specific patterns used as alarms and for the reverse, a distinctive "all-clear" call. Along with vocalization, prairie dogs also have developed different postures and displays that are used for communication, ranging from

Adult prairie dogs not only signal when danger is approaching, they have a unique call that signifies that the danger has passed. This bark is known as a "jump yip," a sharp call often issued while standing on its hind legs.

mutual grooming to a unique mouth-to-mouth "kiss" that serves as a greeting among animals that know each other.

Alarm barks can vary in intensity and frequency. In open ground, the sound of their calls can carry for more than a half mile. The most serious threats produce the loudest alarms and are repeated most frequently. In general, as a threat diminishes, the intensity of

When prairie dogs within a family group meet one another, they practice a unique form of greeting. Standing or sitting, they "kiss," touching their front teeth together. This intimate gesture helps reinforce bonds and makes it harder for animals from outside their group to interlope on their territory.

the bark drops and the frequency slows. At the most intense level, alarm barks may be delivered at the rate of sixty or more per minute. This type of alarm call typically lasts for only a few minutes, followed by a less intense session of calling in which the frequency may be forty or fewer calls per minute. In some cases, the continued presence of a predator or unknown element can trigger an alarm call session that may last for more than an hour.

Because prairie dogs are so social, they depend upon alarm calls for mutual protection. When an alarm call is given by an individual animal, most or all of the other animals in a family group and the entire colony will rush to the entrance of their burrows, close to safety, and add their own calls to the din. But this is not an automatic reaction. Once an initial call has been made, other animals will attempt to locate the source of the threat and only when it has been identified will they join in the chorus.

Biologists have determined that in some colonies, there are individual prairie dogs who seem to have a habit of crying "wolf." That is, they are more prone to giving alarm calls than others, and because their calls do not regularly signify the presence of a serious threat, the other animals in the colony tend to ignore them.

Prairie dogs may respond to threats in different ways, perhaps due to maturity and experience, or possibly because of differences in "personality." Although all adult prairie dogs will recognize the potential threat from a large raptor, a coyote, or human, a few have been noted to utter alarm calls for cattle, rabbits, and even grasshoppers.

Although the alarm barks in general are distinct from other prairie dog calls, they also vary according to what kind of predator is in the area. A raptor alarm call is a two-note bark, with both notes at a high pitch and the second note sustained. When given, unlike some other kinds of alarm calls, all prairie dogs within hearing distance will rush to the safety of their burrows, not waiting to identify the threat for themselves. The same call is used for badgers. Different alarm calls signify predators such as snakes or coyotes.

The opposite of the alarm call is a two-note vocalization that means danger is no longer present. This "all clear" signal, referred to as a "jump yip," is typically uttered while the prairie dog hops up on its hind legs and gives a kind of double salute with its forelegs, throwing them up in the air and down again with vigor. Prairie dogs giving the all clear signal have been known to jump completely off the ground and in some cases, fall over backwards. When one animal gives the call, it is often repeated by others in a colony.

Growling is another vocalization that prairie dogs use. As with other mammals, it generally is used as a threat, to menace intruding neighbors or other animals that are trespassing, such as ground squirrels. Prairie dogs also sometimes snap their teeth together rapidly, producing a chattering sound. It is not known if there is a specific meaning for this communication or whether it has a variety of uses. Other sounds include snarls (similar to growls), low-pitched barks, and whines. Frightened prairie dogs sometimes emit a scream-like call when cornered.

FAMILIES

"Vast cities, with regularly laid streets, are often met with in extensive level spots on the prairie. The inhabitants are, however, not men, but creatures the size of a guinea-pig — rodents — a species of marmot. In their habit of associating together in communities, they put us in mind of the industrious beaver; but they are idle little fellows, evidently liking play better than work."

— William H.G. Kingston (1884, *The Western World*)

Prairie dogs are social animals, always living in groups in the wild. Their colonies consist of dozens, hundreds, or even thousands of family groups, each called a coterie. A coterie consists of a single adult male and one or more adult females; sometimes as many as four females can be part of a coterie. This family group also includes any young offspring that are less than two years old, the age when they leave the family. If all the females in a coterie give birth in the same season and there are a lot of females in the group, the family may have as many as forty members, but this is an extreme. In most coteries, the majority of members are pups and one- to two-year-olds.

Sexual maturity in prairie dogs generally arrives in late winter or early spring during their second year. But sexual maturity and the breeding season are variable, with prairie dogs in southern, warmer latitudes more likely to mature and give birth earlier. The breeding season ranges from January to April at the two extremes, from south to north. Breeding usually happens only once a year, with the female giving birth to a litter of varying size, with one to eight babies being the range.

Mortality is high for young prairie dogs. Disease, predation, and even cannibalism reduce their numbers quickly. By the time young prairie dogs first come up out of their burrows — the average time for first emergence after birth is about forty days — many have already died. On average, only three pups per litter survive to this point.

Despite the many dangers and threats, adult prairie dogs can live for many years. In the wild, individuals have been tracked for five to eight years; in captivity, adults may live even longer, up to ten years or more. Within family groups, group defensiveness usually keeps strangers away, limiting the ability of a group to expand. The adult females within a group are most often related, born into the same litter, or from litters generated by related mothers. Some of the young females may leave as they mature; all of the young males migrate to create their own new family groups.

Prairie dog family groups can be identified when they are above ground feeding. Adults and juveniles graze together within the territory they control.

COLONIES

"If it be an indication of shrewdness and forethought to establish a village nine hundred miles from a railroad, wood, water and grub, and live on alkali and moss agates and wander down the vista of time without a square meal, then the prairie dog is beyond the barest possibility of doubt, keen and shrewd to a wonderful degree."

— Bill Nye (1881, *Bill Nye and Boomerang*)

One of the most distinguishing features of prairie dogs is the congregations in which they live. These colonies can be huge — traditionally extending for miles and consisting of millions of animals — but in modern times are more likely to be small, a few hundred to a few thousand individuals. Prairie dog colonies are also referred to as villages or towns.

In most parts of their remaining range, the black-tailed prairie dog colonies have populations that average forty to fifty acres in size. Before their numbers were decimated, however, individual colonies were typically larger and there were numerous reports of individual colonies of massive size. In north central Kansas, for example, a report from 1859 described a continuous colony that extended from the Saline River to the Solomon River, a distance of more than five miles. In Oklahoma in 1898, a single colony in Canadian County was reportedly twenty-two miles long, and in 1905, one was reported as extending over an estimated 2,500 square miles (6,500 square km).

The largest prairie dog colony on record was reported in 1900 in the high plains section of west Texas. This gigantic concentration was estimated to be about 250 miles long, 100 miles wide, and was home to about 400 million prairie dogs. All of the reports of very large colonies are within the range of the black-tailed prairie dog. Mexican prairie dogs as well have historically produced large colonies. The Utah, Gunnision, and white-tailed species, however, usually produce smaller colonies, a characteristic probably linked to the difference in their habitats.

The scattered colonies that are typical of prairie dog populations today are thought to remain relatively stable in numbers from year to year. In a natural state and unaffected by pressures from hunting, poisoning, or urban sprawl, colonies typically create excess population, which limits the ability of the surrounding environment to supply adequate food. Lack of food, combined with internal pressure, drives some individuals to seek new territory, founding new colonies in the process or repopulating the burrows of colonies that have been abandoned or destroyed.

Black-tailed prairie dogs traditionally migrate under these conditions in May and June, early enough in the summer to find new food and shelter before the upcoming lean months of winter. Prairie dog towns that are decimated by plague or poisoning, but within a general territory inhabited by other colonies, may be completely repopulated due to this kind of movement — including subsequent breeding — within three years.

Within a large colony, most of the residents live completely surrounded by other residents. Only at the edges do individual prairie dog burrows make contact with the "outside world." Some kinds of activities and behaviors differ according to where in the colony an individual prairie dog lives. This includes feeding, finding mates, defending territory, and being susceptible to predators.

The size of a colony is in direct relationship to the ecology of the colony. In some parts of their range, the terrain in and around a prairie dog colony forms natural barriers, effectively forcing a single group to split up into sub-groups. These divisions are referred to as wards. Colonies that have such distinct groups may be divided by rocky outcroppings, steep hills, streams, or even dense stands of tall grasses, brush, or trees.

Within a single colony, frequent traffic from one burrow entrance to another can develop well-marked runways, but prairie dogs usually do not limit themselves to the same passages above ground. Intensive browsing can also create cleared areas that stretch

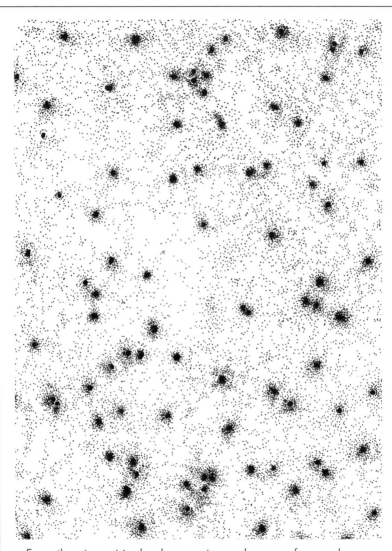

From the air, prairie dog burrows in a colony can form a dense pattern. A single family burrow may have one or more entrances, and one family may have one or more burrows. Within a colony, however, family burrows represent separate territories and are not interconnected.

between burrows. But in older, more established colonies, the overall pattern of vegetation is generally decreased in quantity, reducing the appearance of runways.

The number of burrows in one colony can vary considerably, but the general density in relation to land tends to remain the same. Variations from one colony to another are probably related more to soil conditions than population pressure. In some studies of black-tailed prairie dogs, the average surface space related to one burrow ranged from about 1,700 square feet to about 2,200 square feet. Roughly, that represents a square that is about forty feet per side. For this species, the average density of burrows varies from fifty to sixty per acre, with the densest concentrations in the oldest towns. Other species generally are not as densely populated, with greater space between burrows.

Prairie dogs continually build and expand burrows and move from one burrow to another, making a wide variation in the number of prairie dogs that may reside in one burrow. The result is a lopsided relationship between the number of burrows and the population of a colony.

In one study of colonies in a national park, there were four different zones of habitat identified. These zones each had different types of forage conditions, presumably influencing how many animals and what type of animals lived in each zone. The zones were labeled "old town center," "center," "interior," and "young town edge." Burrows with the longest occupancy were found in the "old town center"; those at the "young town edge" had the shortest. Burrows near the edges of the colonies had on average more young

---

SITE PREFERENCES

Black-tailed prairie dogs generally prefer these characteristics for the location of colonies ...

- Deep soil layers
- Few rocks
- No flooding hazard
- Productive soil types
- Flat land or slopes of less than 9 degrees

per female, most likely due to access to more food and higher quality forage. Not surprisingly, since the vegetation varies among the different zones in a colony, prairie dogs living in the different zones also have somewhat different diets, dependent on the food available to them in their immediate territory.

When prairie dogs move up to several hundred feet away from an established colony, the movement is referred to as colony expansion. This kind of movement gradually expands the area associated with a single colony. When individual prairie dogs move farther away, it is referred to as jump dispersal, in effect a kind of migration. In most cases of prairie dog movements, even up to five miles away from an existing colony, the traveling animals often move to the edges of another existing colony. In some cases, colonies that expand may have as much as 90 percent of their expansion contributed by prairie dogs moving in from other colonies.

Much of the time, prairie dogs on the move are young males, subordinates of older males in a family and driven out to seek new territory in order to find their own mates. A certain amount of territorial aggression also involves migration, with males seeking out abandoned burrows, or those that are not aggressively defended, in order to establish their own territory.

One of the greatest zones for expansion is found at the edges of an existing colony, where expanding families often dig extra burrows in the fall. These newly-constructed burrows are secondary in use to the family's primary burrow and are often abandoned with the coming of winter. But in the spring, the same abandoned burrows offer an opportunity for males traveling in search of territory to call their own. Females may also move from one place to another, but are usually excluded from moving into the center of existing colonies.

When colonies expand, new burrows are often within several hundred feet from the edges of the original colony. This distance offers access to new grazing territory and also provides a necessary link with the protective defenses of the original colony. The animals moving into the new areas are still within visible range of familiar landmarks and most importantly, are within hearing distance of the combined warning system provided by the animals they have left behind, increasing their chances of survival.

Prairie dogs, however, can make more significant moves away from home. There are reports of individual animals and pairs moving from one to several miles away from existing colonies before starting their burrowing activity.

Rare reports also tell of more significant mass movements, in which dozens, hundreds, or even thousands of prairie dogs migrate together across open ground. The trigger for such events is thought to be severe or prolonged drought, eliminating the food supply in an existing colony.

FOOD

"Poor helpless little Yek-yek, he has no friends; his enemies and his list of burdens increase. The prey of everything that preys, he yet seems incapable of any measure of retaliation. The only visible joy in his life is his daily hasty meal of unsucculent grass, gathered between cautious looks around for any new approaching trouble ..."

— Ernest Thompson Seton (1913, *Wild Animals at Home*)

Like all rodents, prairie dogs are often busy gnawing, a necessary activity to keep their incisors from growing too long. But most of the gnawing is aimed at acquiring food, primarily grasses.

Detailed examination of prairie dog diets show that although varied in nature, grasses form the major part. A study of black-tailed prairie dogs in South Dakota revealed that five grasses alone formed the bulk of their intake. These were western wheatgrass, blue grama, buffalo grass, sixweeks fescue, and tumblegrass. For all species of prairie dogs, the grasses that make up the main part of their diet may be consumed wholly, or certain parts selectively chosen, including seed heads, leaves, awns, and stolons. Generally, the stalks are eaten to within an inch or two above the ground. How much do prairie dogs eat? In one year, one cow eats the equivalent of what 256 adult prairie dogs consume.

Prairie dogs, like many rodents, spend much of their active time eating. These animals are herbivores with a diet of vegetation gleaned from the area around their burrows. Located in the treeless plains of the West, most of this vegetation is the typical foliage of the short-grass and mixed-grass prairie.

Prairie dogs will also eat roots, seeds, fruit, buds, and flowers that are encountered within their territory. They have also been observed eating insects, although not usually on a regular basis unless the regular vegetation is limited. In some areas, black-tailed prairie dogs have also been observed eating buffalo dung, both fresh

PRAIRIE DOG PLANT MENU

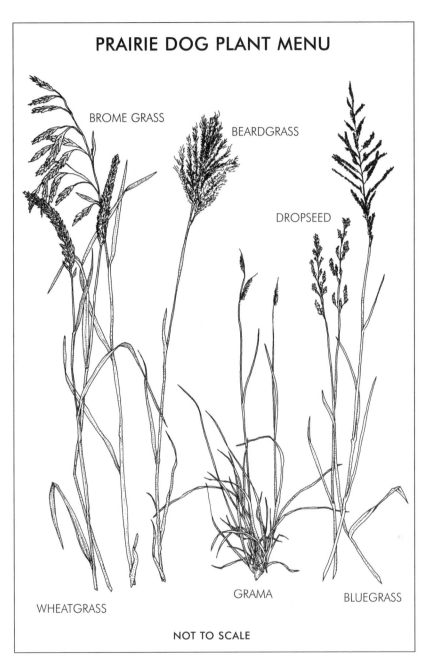

BROME GRASS

BEARDGRASS

DROPSEED

WHEATGRASS

GRAMA

BLUEGRASS

NOT TO SCALE

Prairie dogs generally prefer grasses, but eat a wide variety of plants that grow in their habitats. These include wildflowers, plants some people consider weeds, agricultural crops, and some introduced species, such as the dandelion.

WILD BARLEY

FESCUE

MUHLY

BUFFALO GRASS

NOT TO SCALE

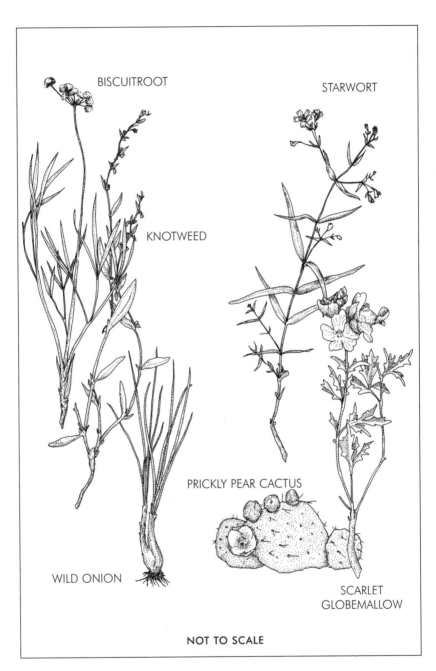

BISCUITROOT

STARWORT

KNOTWEED

PRICKLY PEAR CACTUS

WILD ONION

SCARLET
GLOBEMALLOW

NOT TO SCALE

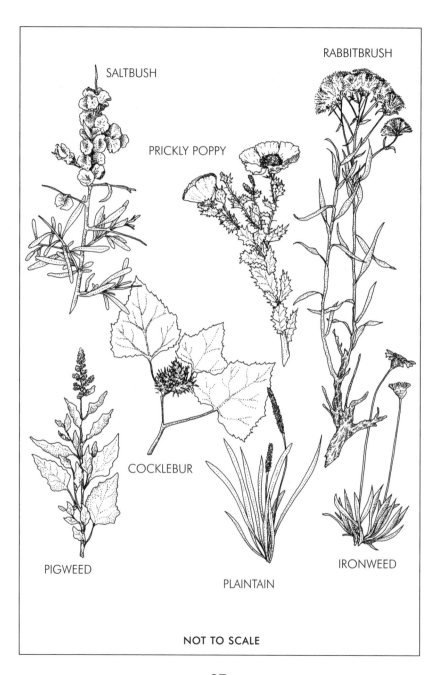

SALTBUSH

RABBITBRUSH

PRICKLY POPPY

PIGWEED

COCKLEBUR

PLAINTAIN

IRONWEED

NOT TO SCALE

and dried. Although they live in close-knit family groups, prairie dogs are also occasionally known to be cannibals, with adult females killing and eating the young of other females. In a few cases, adults have also been known to feed on the carcasses of dead prairie dog adults or juveniles.

At different times of the year, prairie dogs in a specific location will often target different food sources. Major summer food sources are wheatgrass, grama grass, buffalo grass, scarlet globemallow, and rabbitbrush. Major winter food sources are prickly pear cactus, thistles, and roots of different plants. Plants that are not part of the regular diet of prairie dogs include sagebrush, three-awn, the aptly named prairie dog weed (also known simply as dogweed) and horseweed. However, they may eat any of these if other food is scarce.

Prairie dogs can spend a lot of time eating when they are above ground, but they are selective about what they eat. They prefer certain plants to others, select different plants to eat in different seasons, and may target certain plants just for specific plant parts, such as young shoots or leaves.

NOT ON THE MENU

Prairie dogs avoid eating some species of plants. However, this avoidance varies from one part of their range to another. Three-awn, a variety of grass, for example, is not part of the diet for black-tailed prairie dogs, but is eaten by some other species. Also, some plants, such as sagebrush, may be shunned for much of the year, but targeted in the Spring just for its young leaves.

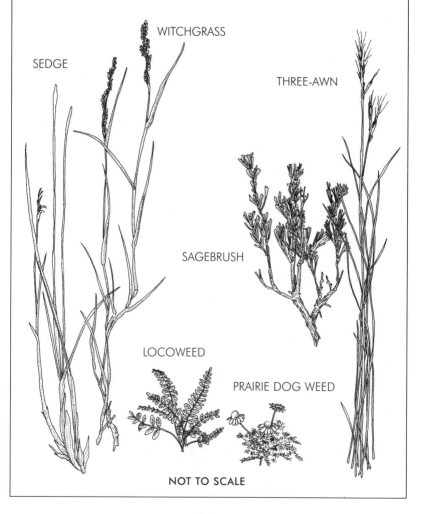

WITCHGRASS

SEDGE

THREE-AWN

SAGEBRUSH

LOCOWEED

PRAIRIE DOG WEED

NOT TO SCALE

In parts of their range in the southwest, one source of food in many colonies is mesquite. Mesquite bushes growing in prairie dog colonies are systematically pruned, with young seedlings a favorite target. Seed pods and bark are also sources of food from mesquite. This has the effect of keeping mesquite groves from expanding too densely, driving out other plant species. When prairie dogs were destroyed in large numbers in the southwest in the early part of the 1900s, this natural restraint on the spread of mesquite was removed, permitting widescale expansion of its territory. In some areas of this region today, where there are no longer any prairie dogs, it is considered a nuisance plant.

Prairie dogs have a lot of dexterity in their front paws, allowing them to grasp and manipulate individual plants as they are eaten. Using their paws in this manner also allows them to eat sitting up, a useful posture that helps them keep an eye out for danger.

DIET VARIETY

Research on prairie dog diets from different areas of their range includes the following plants as part of their regular diet, but this list only partially represents the complete variety of what they may eat.

arrow feather

beardgrass

bentgrass

biscuitroot

blue grama

bluegrass

bluestem wheatgrass

breadroot

brome grass

buffalo grass

cactus

Carolina geranium

cocklebur

curly mesquite

dandelion

devil's claw

dropseed

dwarf morning glory

fescue

foxtail barley

Froelich amaranth

frogfruit

horseweed

Indian ricegrass

ironweed

knotweed

lambsquarters

milkweed

muhly

mullein

needle-and-thread

nightshade

paspalum

peppergrass

phlox

pigweed

Plains wild indigo

prairie sandgrass

prostrate verain

purple poppy mallow

rabbitbrush

ragweed

red three-awn

redtop

saltbush

scarlet butterfly weed

scarlet globe-mallow

sensitive briar

silver beardgrass

skeleton weed

snowberry

spiderwort

spurge

stickseed

Texas croton

thistles

Virginia plantain

western ragweed

wheatgrass

white prickly poppy

wild barley

wild blue indigo

windmill grass

winterfat

wire grass

wirestem muhly

wooly plantain

yellow wood sorrel

In eating grasses, prairie dogs usually nip off a plant near its base, then stand or sit upright, sometimes crouching on three legs, holding the plant with one paw while munching progressively from the bottom end of the cut piece upwards. With some grasses and in some conditions, a prairie dog may appear picky, nipping off grass stalks but only eating a few bites of each before moving on to the next. In many plants that they target, particularly grasses, the most succulent part is near the base and this likely is favored because of the higher water content.

At times, prairie dogs seem to select plants more for the crude fiber and cellulose content rather than moisture or nutrition. And they also occasionally select plants just to cut them down, without eating them. This activity is mostly associated with the removal of taller plants that might help conceal predators.

Adult prairie dogs prepare for winter by putting on extra weight. Feeding activity in the late summer and fall increases in order to fulfill this need. When vegetation is plentiful, this feeding activity can result in significiant gains, sometimes doubling an individual's weight.

While they eat, prairie dogs may concentrate only on one kind of plant, selecting this plant for ingestion over a period of hours, but most of the time, they move from one type of plant to another, continually varying what they eat. From year to year, variation in diet within a particular colony can also happen, possibly because their eating habits may diminish availability of one or more plant species.

Although vegetarian, prairie dogs typically eat small amounts of insects and other animal matter. The majority of this animal intake is accidental, ingested along with the grasses they forage upon, but some kinds of insects, particularly grasshoppers, are deliberately captured and eaten. These insects are usually eaten headfirst.

In the greening days of spring and early summer, prairie dogs select different grasses to eat than later in the summer or fall. This is not necessarily because of taste preferences or because of nutritional content, but a practical response to which grasses and plants are most available in a given season.

In the fall, when dry conditions and cold weather begin to stunt plant growth, the main part of their diet is dried grasses. In the depth of the winter months, roots are also targeted, with digging above ground part of their forage activity.

Prairie dogs are voracious eaters, but they do not eat everything in sight. Except in drought conditions, some vegetation always grows in and around a colony. In fact, in one study of a prairie dog town in Oklahoma, cattle were fenced out to determine how much the prairie dogs themselves affected the plants in their vicinity. Despite normal feeding behavior by the protected rodents, the vegetation grew so dense that the prairie dogs migrated to another area.

In the late winter and early spring, before vegetation begins to appear in abundance, prairie dogs are usually much thinner than at other times of the year. By mid-summer, when heavy feeding is at its peak, they gain a considerable amount of fat, often appearing obese. This fat is an essential reserve of energy needed during the lean days of winter.

Water is a critical part of the diet of all animals, but it is in short supply throughout much of the prairie dogs' range. In many colonies, the chief source of water comes from plant material, with succulent stems and leaves a favorite food source. In fact, some long-time observers of prairie dog colonies have noted that they never seem to take advantage of standing water after rainstorms, ignoring this resource. The winter months provide much of the precipitation in parts of their range, and during winter months when snow is on the ground, female prairie dogs have been observed eating it frequently, perhaps a response to the increased need for water when pregnant or lactating.

HABITAT

"These little fellows select for their towns a level piece of prairie, with a sandy or gravelly soil, out of which they can excavate their dwellings with great facility. Being of a very sociable disposition, they choose to live in a large community, where laws exist for the public good; and there is less danger to be apprehended from the attacks of their numerous and crafty enemies."

— Henry Howe (1857, *Historical Collections of the Great West*)

Prairie dogs have adapted to thrive in a prairie environment. From the choice of food to their burrows, the type of land that is most suitable for their colonies is characterized by the treeless plains that cover most of the territory in the western United States. Yet this is a complex relationship, for prairie dogs only thrive where grazing animals such as bison are also present. The initial grazing by these herbivores prepares the way for the prairie dogs, reducing high grasses and other unwanted plants, creating opportunity for the kinds of shorter grasses that prairie dogs prefer and at the same time, eliminating ground cover that might hide predators. The hooved visitors also leave behind large amounts of dung, a natural fertilizer that aids in the growth of vegetation.

Until about one hundred fifty years ago, bison and antelope were the dominant grazing animals on the prairie and were chiefly responsible for creating ideal habitat for prairie dogs. Aggressive over-hunting eliminated the bison but it also marked the beginning of a new era, the introduction of domesticated cattle to the West. For at least the past one hundred years, cattle have been the dominant grazing animal, probably triggering a rapid expansion of prairie dog numbers, at least until major poisoning programs created a dramatic reduction.

As prairie dogs eat, they reduce the height of the vegetation surrounding their burrows. They rarely chew plants completely to the ground, but selectively remove stalks and vegetation down to a shorter height, triggering re-growth activity in the plants. In fact, prairie dog colonies are characterized by vegetation that is in an early, active stage of growth, typically generating more nutrients than plants that are more mature.

By keeping the vegetation "mowed," the amount of bare ground that is exposed increases, providing more productive foraging for animals and birds that rely on seeds. And as taller grasses are reduced in height, the altered density and availability of light favors another class of plant known as forbs — wild legumes and broad-leafed plants — which, in turn, provide cover and food for other animals.

The constant burrowing activity of prairie dogs is in itself a force that alters the habitat. Bringing up soil from under the surface acts as a mixing influence, helping to build soil quality over time. Biologists refer to this kind of soil distribution as bioturbation.

Although ranchers traditionally believed that prairie dogs significantly reduced the amount of vegetation available to livestock, the overall effect in volume is not much, less than ten percent. And in reality their eating preferences keeps grasses — the favorite food of most grazing animals, including cattle — shorter but more nutritious, as it triggers rapid growth cycles in these plants. In natural conditions, prairie dog colonies are favored grazing sites for bison and antelope — and cattle as well — because these herd animals instinctively recognize the increased food value of the grasses found there. Another benefit from the activities of prairie dogs is greater retention of moisture in the soil within their colonies, keeping vegetation within these bounds greener longer in the season, even as dry summer conditions wither surrounding grasslands.

In turn, grazing animals perform a function that is useful for the prairie dogs. Moving around in larger areas than the prairie dogs themselves, these grazers also target taller grasses and other vegetation that can hide predators looking for an easy meal. While prairie dogs are more likely to inhabit areas within short and mixed-grass prairies, grazing herds of bison, antelope, and cattle make it possible for them to move into less perfect terrain, the tall-grass prairie. The vegetation around prairie dog burrows is typically short, ranging from two to five inches in height (5 to 13 cm).

In a few cases in modern times, prairie dog colonies have been located in terrain that doesn't fit the ideal of the traditional prairie. Due to pressure created by expanding cities or overgrazing livestock, a few colonies have been situated in groves of cottonwood trees or stands of shrubs or other trees. Sagebrush, common throughout large sections of the West, has also occasionally been invaded by prairie dogs, although with their presence, this brushy vegetation is quickly chewed down.

Flat terrain is the preference when it comes to prairie dog burrows. Yet the nature of the western landscape means that much of their burrowing must be done on less-than-level ground. Studies of prairie dog colonies in Colorado indicate sloping colonies are most often less than twelve degrees, with nine degrees being an average extreme; in South Dakota, slopes may be steeper, even up to forty-five degrees.

Soil type is critical for the location of prairie dog colonies, if only because they require suitable digging conditions for their extensive burrows. Ideally, colonies are situated where the soil is well drained, as this kind of condition helps retain moisture, and moisture content is important in maintaining stability in the walls of burrows. However, prairie dog towns have been found with a wide variety of soil conditions present, including clay and sand, although the latter is not a favored addition. In rare cases, prairie dogs may also extend their burrowing activity to soft rock, such as shale, in order to gain the length and depth necessary for safety. Yet in most cases, rocks and rocky conditions are avoided. Because most burrows range from five to fifteen feet in depth, the habitat best suited to prairie dogs features soil depths that permit burrowing within this range.

BURROWS

"In the winter, when the prairie dog, snug in his subterranean abode, and with granaries well filled, never cares to expose his little nose to the icy blasts which sweep across the plains, but between eating and sleeping, passes merrily the long frozen winter, he is often roused from his warm bed, and almost congealed with terror while hearing the snorting yelp of the half-famished wolf, who, mad with hunger, assaults with tooth and claw, the frost-bound roof of his house, and with almost superlupine strength, hurls down the well cemented walls, tears up the passages, plunges his cold nose into the very chambers, snorts into them with ravenous anxiety, and drives the poor little trembling inmate into the most remote corners, too often to be dragged forth and unhesitatingly devoured."

— Henry Howe (1857, *Historical Collections of the Great West*)

Much as beaver lodges are closely linked to beavers, so too are prairie dog burrows linked to prairie dogs. One cannot exist without the other. The burrow is not only the residence for prairie dogs, it is a refuge from danger, a protective barrier against extremes of heat and cold, and a safe structure in which to rear new generations.

Prairie dog burrows are usually located in areas where the soil is appropriate for digging and maintaining open tunnels. Well-drained soil is the best type, with enough moisture present to allow tunnel walls to hold their shape. Sandy soil and heavy deposits of clay discourage prairie dogs, but may be targeted if better opportunities are not available. Soft rock may also be present, with digging and chewing used to produce passageways.

As prairie dogs dig, they mostly use their front paws, which are equipped with strong claws. Displaced soil is usually pushed backward, eventually ending up expelled through a tunnel entrance, cre-

Elevated burrow entrances are formed from the dirt excavated when burrows are being dug. This material can be formed into mounds, with the prairie dogs using their noses, heads, and paws to pack the material into place.

Another kind of entrance is the cone, with looser material spilling out and away from the burrow.

Secondary entrances are often dug out from below, with little or no soil excavated to form a mound.

ating a mound. As tunnels extend deeper into the ground, a combination of kicking from the front and back legs is used to move the soil upward and outward. The animals may also push soil forward with their forelegs.

Usually, one prairie dog does the digging for a burrow, but sometimes more than one will be involved, with each trading off digging

The members of a prairie dog family sometimes collect plant material and carry it into the nesting chambers inside their burrows.

duties. Often, the greatest burrow building activity will be in the spring or early summer when the soil contains more moisture, making it easier to work with. After a rain, building and repair activity will also increase, also because of the moisture factor.

As soil is expelled from a burrow entrance, a mound gradually rises around the opening. Prairie dogs will use their noses, mouths, and front legs to pack this material down, to keep it from falling back into the burrow. After rains, they may also take advantage of the wet conditions to do a little added tamping.

A single prairie dog burrow will have two or more openings; some have as many as five or six. The added entrances are critical for several reasons. They provide options for prairie dogs rushing for safety when attacked by predators; they provide options for prairie dogs being chased in their own burrow system by ferrets, snakes, or badgers; and they provide a natural system of ventilation.

The entrances to burrows can vary considerably in style. Some are at the center of large mounds, others open inconspicuously. Some entrances are dug almost straight down for as much as five or six feet before tunneling off at a less acute angle, and some slant down at a more gentle slope. The slope of slanting burrows is usually from fifteen to twenty-five degrees.

Mounds have the primary function of increasing ventilation by creating a barrier for air blowing across the ground. As air rises and passes over a mound, the air pressure inside is lowered, creating a small but effective force that pulls air in through other entrances, ventilating the entire burrow complex.

BURROW CHARACTERISTICS

Black-tailed prairie dogs construct burrows with these typical features ...

- 2 entrances per burrow
- Depth of 3–10 feet
- Total length of 50 feet
- Diameter of 4–5 inches
- Entrance mound 3–6 feet in diameter

Mounds are also a useful elevated platform for observation and can help channel surface water away from a burrow entrance.

Where colonies spread over sloping ground, burrow openings tend to head into the ground directly away from the face of the slope; east-facing hills have burrows running to the west and opening to the east, for example. But this does not appear to be a rigid rule for prairie dogs, and other orientations are also present. On level ground, there is a lot of variation in the direction that burrow openings face.

Although most of the material in a mound may come from the soil displaced during digging, additional material is also added. This

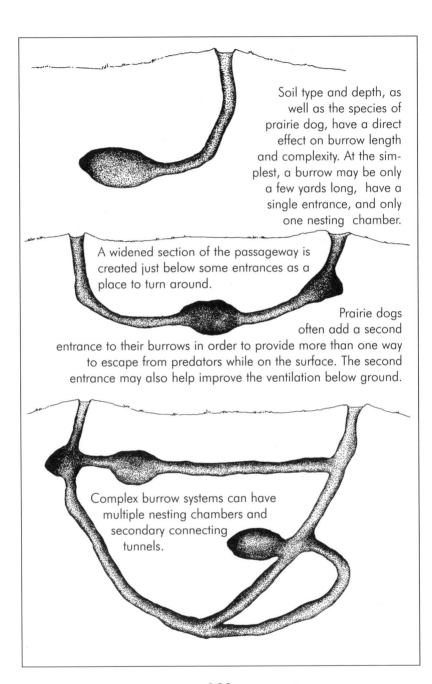

Soil type and depth, as well as the species of prairie dog, have a direct effect on burrow length and complexity. At the simplest, a burrow may be only a few yards long, have a single entrance, and only one nesting chamber.

A widened section of the passageway is created just below some entrances as a place to turn around.

Prairie dogs often add a second entrance to their burrows in order to provide more than one way to escape from predators while on the surface. The second entrance may also help improve the ventilation below ground.

Complex burrow systems can have multiple nesting chambers and secondary connecting tunnels.

comes from the ground surrounding the burrow entrance. The burrow inhabitants will scrape and push loose dirt and plant material up into the slopes of the entrance mound, packing it down with their noses and foreheads. Prairie dog mounds sometimes have a distinct pattern in their surface, a pattern created by noseprints made in damp soil.

Vertical entrances, which are dug from underneath (as an extension of an existing burrow) do not generate any material from which a mound might be made, but some prairie dogs will construct a simple cone-shaped rim anyway, scraping soil from the surrounding surface. In some cases, soil scraped away to add to a mound may create a slight depression circling the area, the result of the soil being removed from the surface.

After weeks or months of existence, the mounds often get efficiently compressed. Over time, the drying effect of the sun and constant tamping can turn these mounds into hard-packed structures that can last long after a burrow is abandoned.

With good soil conditions present, prairie dog mounds can vary in height from one to three feet and extend up to ten feet in diameter, with typical diameters between three and six feet. Yet not all prairie dog burrows or colonies feature prominent mounds. If the local climate or weather conditions create a sufficient reduction in soil moisture, the result is a colony whose burrows plunge more or less directly into the ground. Here, as prairie dogs excavate new burrows and perform normal housekeeping services, the loose soil that is kicked up to the surface does not have enough binding properties to form mounds, instead spreading out over the surface or blowing away.

In practice, the first burrow a prairie dog digs in a location will feature a slanting entrance. Additional entrances to a burrow system can include vertical tunnels exiting to the surface; these are dug from the bottom up. The soil that is displaced during this operation is kicked back out through another hole.

Various rooms and widened structures are included within a typical burrow system. In some cases, the local residents may even seal up an entrance or room, possibly to cut off access to a dead family member. A few feet into a burrow from a major entrance, a widened spot is created, a useful facility for turning around. Deep within a burrow system, larger chambers are excavated for sleeping and raising young. These may be lined with dried grasses, collected and carried inside in large quantities; all members of a family participate in this gathering activity. Nesting and sleeping chambers are eighteen to twenty-four inches in diameter and twelve to fifteen inches high.

In some burrow systems, branching tunnels provide multiple connections between underground sites; some tunnels may also lead nowhere, dead-ends that serve no known purpose. Midden heaps are also a feature of burrows. These underground piles are located in special rooms and contain scraps of food, other organic debris, feces, and loose soil or rocks. But unlike other rodents — beavers, for example — prairie dogs do not create stashes of food inside their burrows.

In many, if not most colonies, sloping tunnels and vertical entrances lead to an underground system that is more or less horizontal. The tunnels that form this system may branch and meander, but they often follow the same layer of soil, a practical advantage to the diggers, who may encounter gravel, rocks, or more difficult material at deeper or shallower levels.

At the edges of a prairie dog colony, residents often move out of existing burrows and dig new ones. Moving from one burrow to another may be a survival instinct, keeping predators from finding easy targets. It may also help reduce the number of parasites, such as fleas, which build up over time in a burrow that is in continual use.

Moving also helps extend colonies deeper into the surrounding territory, where food may be more plentiful. Observers have noted that initially, prairie dogs extending their territory may dig only shallow burrows, returning to their original, deeper burrows in winter. Over time, if the vegetation and soil type meets the requirements of the animals, more permanent burrows are created in the new territory.

Although burrow lengths may vary, a typical length is roughly fifty feet. The average burrow diameter is four to five inches. Depths of up to fifteen feet have been reported for a few burrows, although this is an extreme. Most of the time, burrows run horizontally in a zone three to six feet down. Based on an average burrow diameter and length, prairie dogs must excavate about six cubic feet (0.17 cubic m.) of soil in construction activity.

Even though prairie dogs may not hesitate to leave their burrows and construct new ones, in some colonies there are burrows in use for long periods of time, passing through many generations. Some biologists speculate that there could be burrows that have been in use for hundreds of years. Evidence of even older burrows have also been found, with the underground passageways filled in with foreign material, creating a kind of "petrified" effect.

Prairie dog colonies will have thirty to fifty burrow entrances per acre, with the number varying according to population density, soil type, and the general type of terrain. There are also slight differences in mound styles and burrow density from species to species, although this may be as much due to terrain differences as instinctive building behavior. While cone-shaped burrows are the characteristic of black-tailed prairie dogs, these entrance shapes are not shared by the white-tailed prairie dog. The range of the latter corresponds to a hillier, more rocky terrain and these animals typically dig their tunnels on hillsides, not flat ground.

Burrows of the white-tailed prairie dog usually open directly into the ground; the earth that is excavated is scattered on the downhill side, and sometimes formed into flattened entrance platforms, handy for basking in the sun if not built high enough to provide an advantage when searching for predators. The soil conditions found throughout the range of the white-tailed prairie dog also limits the size and length of the tunnels, which average only about six feet in length or depth.

Prairie dog burrows not only provide home and shelter for the prairie dogs that built them, other animals as well find refuge here. Box turtles, for example, frequently nest in burrows and may even hibernate there. Snakes also seek out burrows as nesting chambers, resting sites, and hibernation dens. This includes rattlers and bull snakes, which may prey on prairie dogs, but other, non-threatening snakes are also found, including the western hog-nose and lined snakes. Ground squirrels are often found in abundance around

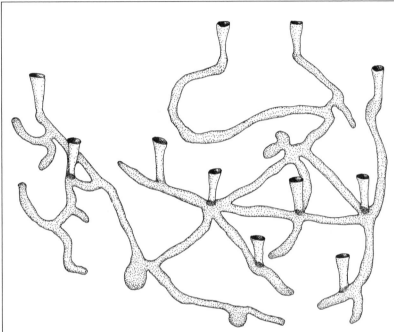

In this schematic of a complex burrow system, there are multiple entrances and connecting passageways. Burrows that are used for many generations create opportunities for the residents to continuously modify their living quarters, sometimes to add room as a family expands. Passageways, chambers, and even entrances may also be plugged with dirt and debris, further modifying a burrow system. Sometimes burrow extensions are abandoned, creating dead ends. In most cases, even when burrow systems are complex, the passageways usually remain roughly horizontal, but layers of rock or dense material can create natural barriers, forcing variations in depth.

prairie dog colonies, but these rodents usually dig their own burrows. In addition, some species of spiders and insects are attracted to these dark holes in the ground.

Another relationship between prairie dog mounds and the local animal community arises from their attractiveness to herd animals such as bison, antelope, elk, mule deer, and domestic cattle. The bare piles of dirt give the herd animals an opportunity for dust baths, an activity that helps remove parasites.

PREDATORS

"The prairie dog leads a life of constant alarm, and numerous enemies are ever on the watch to surprise him. The hawk and the eagle, hovering high in air, watch their towns, and pounce suddenly upon them, never failing to carry off in their talons some unhappy member of the community. The coyote, too, a hereditary foe, lurks behind a hillock, watching patiently for hours, until an unlucky straggler approaches within reach of his murderous spring."

— Henry Howe (1857, *Historical Collections of the Great West*)

As a relatively small rodent, a prairie dog is a potential meal to a wide variety of flying, loping, and crawling predators. Coyotes, bobcats, black-footed ferrets, weasels, badgers, red foxes, gray foxes, mountain lions, and grizzly bears are among those hunting for a meal on the ground. Although wolves are now gone from almost the entire prairie dog range, they were a traditional predator as well. Snakes that target prairie dogs include several species of rattlesnakes and bull snakes.

Raptors that feed on prairie dogs include golden eagles, bald eagles, northern harriers, prairie falcons, red-tailed hawks, peregrine falcons, accipiter hawks, Cooper's hawks, great horned owls, and buteos. Burrowing owls, which are common residents of prairie dog colonies, mostly feed on insects and smaller rodents, but have been known to occasionally catch small adult prairie dogs, juveniles, and pups.

Despite the variety of threats, most predation in prairie dog colonies is concentrated in only a few species of animals. Badgers are possibly the most prolific prairie dog hunters, digging up burrows and killing entire families. Coyotes are also frequent visitors to colonies, and in parts of the prairie dog range, they target these animals as a constant source of food.

The black-footed ferret, however, is the one predator that is most closely linked to prairie dogs. Although once driven close to extinction, these wily predators have evolved to live inside prairie dog burrows and target them almost exclusively as a source of food.

Living at the tail end of the food chain makes prairie dogs very vigilant. Their senses and sophisticated system of communication aid in identifying and responding to their predators. As much as half of all time above ground can be occupied with searching for danger. Amid this protective activity, prairie dogs have learned to live in close proximity to animals that do not pose a threat to them. These include grazing herd animals such as bison, antelope, and cattle, as well as many species of birds, smaller rodents, rabbits, and small reptiles.

Prairie dogs are not well equipped to defend themselves against predators, relying instead on wariness and the defense of their burrows. But when cornered, individual prairie dogs may gnash their incisors, lunge at their attackers, and are capable of inflicting serious wounds with their teeth.

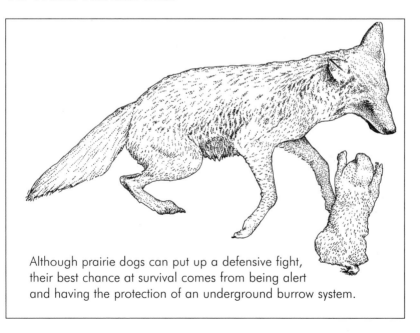

Although prairie dogs can put up a defensive fight, their best chance at survival comes from being alert and having the protection of an underground burrow system.

MAJOR PRAIRIE DOG PREDATORS

Along with this representative selection, prairie dogs are hunted and eaten by other carnivores and raptors as well as domestic dogs and cats. They are also targeted by human hunters for sport in some states.

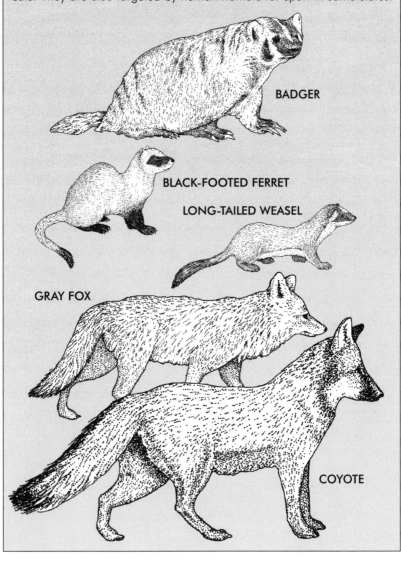

BADGER

BLACK-FOOTED FERRET

LONG-TAILED WEASEL

GRAY FOX

COYOTE

FERRUGINOUS HAWK

RED-TAILED HAWK

GOLDEN EAGLE

RATTLESNAKE

Although rattlesnakes are thought to target prairie dogs, only the largest of this species can manage to kill and swallow an adult prairie dog. The presence of these snakes in prairie dog colonies may be because they mostly hunt for smaller juveniles and young pups. In fact, biologists have noted that in the northern part of the prairie dog range, the birth of pups is generally when rattlesnakes are hibernating, perhaps an evolutionary response to this threat. For most rattlesnakes, hunting is good in prairie dog colonies, not only because of the prairie dogs, but because their burrows and the alteration of the local landscape make them great breeding grounds for smaller, more manageable rodents. The same is likely true of bull snakes.

Observers have also noted that in many colonies, prairie dogs do not respond to the presence of snakes the same way as other predators. In some cases, visiting rattlesnakes and bull snakes are completely ignored, with no alarm calls or disruption in feeding activity.

Despite the danger from predators, their threat is not constant year round. During the summer months when the entire population of a colony may be on the surface feeding, the combined alertness of all the animals and the ease of feeding close to their burrows due to the abundance of food, makes it harder for predators to catch them.

During the winter, when individual prairie dogs may venture out alone on the snow, it's a different story. This may be the time of year when attacks by eagles and hawks are most effective. At the end of the summer or during droughts, prairie dogs have to venture farther from their burrows to find vegetation, and this puts them at greater risk. This is the period when they may migrate singly or in large numbers, rambling awkwardly for long distances along the ground and exposing themselves to attack. During territorial disputes, individual prairie dogs may also be forced from their burrows, once again pushed away from their safe haven and made more vulnerable to predators.

When prairie dogs existed in huge numbers throughout their range, they provided a significant source of food for predators, supporting a complex food chain. The widespread destruction of prairie dog colonies in the twentieth century, however, has played a major role in the disruption of this predator-prey relationship, with the near-complete disappearance of the black-footed ferret only the most visible result.

There may be no way to accurately measure just how different the grasslands ecosystem must have been, but some clues exist now that present a picture of just what happens when a large chunk of the food chain disappears. For example, during an outbreak of plague in a highly studied population of black-tailed prairie dogs in central Colorado, several colonies were completely wiped out. As a consequence of this disappearance in their food supply, the population of ferruginous hawks in the area declined by 90 percent. Ferruginous hawks are also being affected by the declining populations of Mexican prairie dogs, as their range is the southern part of the hawks' winter migratory route.

PROFILE OF A PREDATOR: BLACK-FOOTED FERRET

"It is delightful, during fine weather, to see these lively little creatures sporting about the entrance of their burrows, which are always kept in the neatest repair, and are often inhabited by several individuals. When alarmed, they immediately take refuge in their subterranean chambers; or if the dreaded danger be not immediately impending, they stand near the brink of the entrance, bravely barking and flourishing their tails, or else sit erect to reconnoitre the movements of the Enemy."

— Charles Lucien Bonaparte (1831, *American Ornithology*)

The relationship between prairie dogs and black-footed ferrets is one of the most unique among predators and prey. Over a long period of time, this species of ferret evolved to depend on prairie dogs, living and feeding almost exclusively on them. Following the massive destruction of prairie dog colonies in the early part of the 1900s, the ferrets' food source disappeared, and the species almost disappeared along with it.

The black-footed ferret is now considered the rarest mammal in North America. In 1964, it was expected that this animal would be declared extinct, as none had been spotted for several years. But that year, a few ferrets were discovered in a prairie dog colony in Mellette County, South Dakota, triggering an extensive research and observation program, resulting in an effort to capture and raise specimens in captivity. Only eighteen specimens were known to exist in 1986. Since then, several hundred have been raised and dozens have already been reintroduced into natural habitats where their food source, prairie dogs, are protected.

Black-footed ferrets not only depend on prairie dogs as their food supply, they use prairie dog burrows as their dens. Breeding, resting, and feeding usually take place there. When raising their young, adult ferrets will drag the bodies of prairie dogs they have killed over considerable distances to be consumed in the safety of the den.

Adult black-footed ferrets are mostly solitary, getting together only to mate. But in some instances, single prairie dog colonies have been home to dozens of these predators, indicating that they can live as neighbors while competing for food.

Litter size for these ferrets ranges from one to six kits. Female ferrets are protective mothers, guarding and nursing their young inside the protection of abandoned burrows. Offspring mature quickly and the new generation may strike out on their own within only a few months after birth. Typically, the males of this species are more likely to move into new territory, seeking mates.

These ferrets are small compared to their prey. Adult prairie dogs are usually at least the same size and weight as the ferrets, and larger adults may outweigh their attackers considerably. Ferrets stalk their prey at night, venturing into the dark tunnels where prairie dogs are resting. In the wild, black-footed ferrets are thought to only hunt and kill prairie dogs underground, never on the surface. Using their sensitive noses and the ability to feel their way around in the dark, sleeping prairie dogs are tracked down and once located, pounced upon. Ferrets have sharp, dagger-like canine teeth designed for this attack.

They typically bite their prey at the back of the neck and hold on, using these teeth and strong gripping power to inflict a fatal wound. In the killing struggle, the fatal bite may also end up puncturing the prairie dog's throat. Prairie dogs do not always fall victim to this attacking force; in some instances, adult animals will respond to an attack by fighting back and are sometimes able to drive off the attacker. Even though this defense is rarely successful, ferrets have been injured during their hunting forays.

When conditions are normal, an adult black-footed ferret will hunt and kill several times a week, one prairie dog per hunting session. When nursing, mother ferrets may be more active, killing and eating a prairie dog about every other day. In order to maintain a

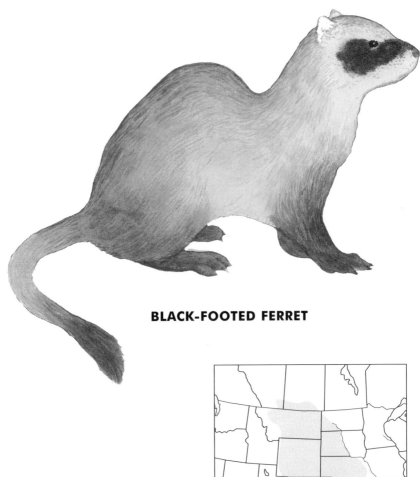

BLACK-FOOTED FERRET

RANGE

Approximate traditional
range of species. Currently
listed as endangered and
not found in the wild except
for a few restoration areas.

VITAL STATISTICS

NAME	**Black-footed ferret** *Mustela nigripes* **SPANISH** hurón de patas negras **FRENCH** putois à pieds noirs
DESCRIPTION	Long, narrow body and long, narrow tail; head short and broad with blunt nose and rounded ears. Color light brown to yellow-brown, darker on back and lighter underneath; dark to black feet; white to pale areas on throat, head, and muzzle; distinctive white to pale face with black mask on forehead; tail marked with black tip. Hair on coat is short and retains the same color throughout the year. Males larger than females.
COMPARISON	Larger than weasels or mink; distinctive black feet and mask not found on weasels or mink.

TOTAL LENGTH	20–24 inches (51–61 cm)	**TAIL LENGTH**	5–6 inches (13–15 cm)

WEIGHT	18–22 ounces (510–624 gm)
TEETH	34 teeth total: incisors 3/3; canines 1/1; premolars 3/3; molars 1/2.
HABITAT	Short and mixed-grass prairies. Traditional favored habitat is within prairie dog colonies.
RANGE	Traditional range within the Great Plains, from extreme southern Saskatchewan and Alberta in the north to northern Texas and New Mexico in the south.
ACTIVITY	Mostly nocturnal. Young born in late spring; 1–6 kits per litter. Feeds primarily on prairie dogs, but also consumes small rodents, birds, and reptiles. Extremely rare; listed as endangered species.

117

healthy balance between predator and prey, scientists believe that a single adult ferret requires a prairie dog colony of at least 100 acres. One study of the diet of black-footed ferrets in the wild concluded that an estimated 109 prairie dogs were needed to feed one female ferret and an average litter during a single year. Other estimates suggest that one ferret family requires from 762 to as many as 2,000 prairie dogs annually for survival.

Black-footed ferrets are vulnerable not only because of the reduced population of their prey, but because they are susceptible to a deadly disease, distemper, which is carried by many domestic animals. While caring for captive ferrets, efforts were taken to protect them from this disease with existing vaccines, but some of the captive ferrets died from a reaction to the medicine. The original captive group also had difficulty reproducing, and all of the original captive group had died by 1979. An additional group of wild ferrets was discovered near Meetettse, Wyoming, in 1981, leading to the now successful program to rear and reintroduce black-footed ferrets into the wild.

Despite being ferocious and skilled hunters of prairie dogs, black-footed ferrets are also vulnerable themselves to larger predators. Great horned owls and coyotes are both known to target ferrets, catching them at night while they are above ground moving from burrow to burrow or when they seek new territory. Other known predators include domestic dogs, cats, and badgers.

The breeding season for black-footed ferrets is March and April, coinciding with the beginning of the most active feeding period for prairie dogs. Females are sexually mature when only one year old. Female ferrets can be choosy about their mating partners but do not depend on males for anything other than mating. The birth and raising of young are entirely managed by the females.

The gestation period for black-footed ferrets is about six weeks and the average size of a litter is 3.3 kits. Born with closed eyes and totally dependent on their mother for warmth and milk, they grow quickly, beginning to eat the meat brought to the burrow by their mother about a month after birth.

Young ferrets reach adult size quickly, usually by the end of the summer, about twelve weeks after birth. As they grow, their mother will initially drag fresh-killed prairie dogs back to the nest chamber as a source of food. As the kits become more mobile and coordinated, this behavior shifts, with the mother leading them to a distant burrow where a fresh-killed carcass has been stashed.

In the wild, black-footed ferrets establish and maintain territories within prairie dog colonies. Boundaries are marked by spraying or rubbing an oily scent from their anal glands; urine and feces are also part of this marking behavior. Ferrets may occasionally fight to defend or acquire territory, but the establishment of boundaries through scent marking creates a more effective and less dangerous method of dealing with competition.

Black-footed ferrets, despite their dependence on prairie dogs, sometimes target other prey animals. Several studies of ferrets in black-tailed and white-tailed prairie dog colonies showed that about 10 percent of their diet may include other small mammals, including mice, voles, and rabbits.

THE ECOLOGY OF PRAIRIE DOG COLONIES

"Approaching a 'village,' the little dogs may be observed frisking about the 'streets' — passing from dwelling to dwelling apparently on visits — sometimes a few clustered together as though in council — here feeding upon the tender herbage — there cleansing their 'houses' or brushing the little hillocks about the door — yet all quiet."

— Josiah Gregg (1845, *Commerce of the Prairies*)

Even though prairie dogs are at the bottom of a food chain, they exert tremendous influence on the environment in which they live. The variety and abundance of plants, insects, and other animals are intertwined with the altered habitat created by the prairie dogs and their colonies.

Vegetation is one of the most visible links to their activity. Prairie dogs are selective in what they eat — preferring plants such as grasses — and keep such plants closely pruned in their feeding activity. In turn, this kind of selective foraging alters their landscape in comparison to the surrounding grassland. As one species of plant is reduced, others move in to replace it. As taller grasses are removed, for example, leafy forbs and legumes thrive.

Plains habitats frequented by prairie dogs are typically found in areas of low rainfall. But the grazing and burrowing activity of these animals helps conserve water by channeling rainfall into underground aquifers and protected layers of soil and rock, reducing the effects of droughts and dry seasons. The amount of vegetation consumed by their foraging also affects this water storage because it reduces the amount of evaporation from leaf surfaces, leaving more moisture in the soil.

Together, this effect helps keep colonies greener later in the year, prolonging the food supply for the prairie dogs that live there. At

Bison are attracted to the altered vegetation found in prairie dog colonies, but they also find these sites useful for another reason. Bare patches of ground created by the prairie dogs provide a natural surface for rolling in dirt, an activity that helps reduce parasites. Continued rolling at the same spots create shallow depressions called wallows.

the same time, the increased nutrition represented by this late season vegetation attracts and sustains other animals dependent on it for survival, including bison, antelope, and even domestic cattle. The open areas where vegetation has been clipped close to the ground also has another attraction for animals such as bison: the bare ground invites dust baths, and the open areas are favored for rutting and resting.

Constant foraging on plants in the colony keeps plants in a constant state of regeneration. Plants that are affected by this kind of grazing activity typically have more nutritive value than older, mature plants, generating a higher quality of food. This benefits prairie dogs but it also is a factor in attracting other grazing animals — among them bison, antelope, deer, and domestic cattle — to such a site.

The burrowing activity of the prairie dogs also contributes to the health and vitality of the soil, mixing organic materials from one

BIRDS ASSOCIATED WITH PRAIRIE DOG COLONIES

More than a hundred bird species have been linked to prairie dog colonies, including raptors that depend on colonies year-round for a source of food and songbirds that drift through during migrations. Associations may include strong dependence, such as with the burrowing owl or a casual link during temporary situations, as when rainstorms produce standing pools of water around the burrows, a lure for waterfowl.

American avocet
American crow
American goldfinch
American kestrel
American magpie
American robin
Baird's sandpiper
Baird's sparrow
bald eagle
barn swallow
black-billed magpie
blue jay
boat-tailed grackle
bobolink
Brewer's blackbird
Brewer's sparrow
brown-headed cowbird
buff-breasted sandpiper
Bullock's oriole
burrowing owl
Cassin's kingbird
Cassin's sparrow
chestnut-collared longspur
Chihuahuan raven
chipping sparrow
cliff swallow

common grackle
common nighthawk
common raven
common redpoll
common yellowthroat
crested caracara
curved-billed thrasher
dickcissel
eastern bluebird
eastern kingbird
eastern meadowlark
European starling

ferruginous hawk
golden eagle
grasshopper sparrow
gray catbird
great horned owl
greater yellowlegs

horned lark
house sparrow
killdeer
Lapland longspur
lark bunting
lark sparrow

larkspur
lesser golden plover
lesser prairie chicken
lesser yellowlegs
loggerhead shrike
long-billed curlew
long-billed dowitcher
marbled godwit
McCown's longspur
meadowlark
merlin
Mississippi kite
mountain bluebird
mountain plover
mourning dove
northern bobwhite
northern flicker
northern harrier
northern mockingbird
northern rough-winged swallow
northern shrike

Oregon junco
pine siskin
prairie chicken
prairie falcon
red-tailed hawk
red-winged blackbird
ring-necked pheasant
rock dove
rough-legged hawk
sage grouse
sage thrasher
Savannah sparrow
Say's phoebe
scaled quail
scissor-tailed flycatcher
sharp-shinned hawk
sharp-tailed grouse
short-eared owl
snow bunting
snowy owl
slate-colored junco
spotted towhee
Sprague's pipit
Swainson's hawk
turkey vulture
vesper sparrow
violet-green swallow
water pipit
western kingbird
western meadowlark
western tanager
white-crowned sparrow
willet
Wilson's phalarope
yellow warbler
yellow-breasted chat
yellow-headed blackbird

layer with inorganic materials from another. This has the effect of producing richer growing conditions for plants. Such mixing also aerates compacted soil, further improving growing conditions. And while they dig and forage, prairie dogs also provide excrement that enriches the local soil, adding to the overall organic content. Compared to surrounding grasslands, the soil in prairie dog colonies has been found to be richer in nitrogen, phosphorus, and organic matter.

The mix of plants associated with colonies along with the reduction in foliage density produce an ecosystem different than the surrounding grasslands, which is a major factor in attracting wildlife. As species move in and become dependent on the habitat associated with the colonies, predators follow their prey and the entire population of animals shifts.

Among the most visible in this wildlife shift are birds. Raptors, for one, are often found in higher concentrations in the vicinity, looking for a meal among the large concentration of prairie dogs. Bald eagles, golden eagles, ferruginous hawks, and red-tailed hawks frequently target prairie dogs, and during the winter months these rodents may form a major part of the diet of these birds wintering in an area.

These large winged predators make regular visits over prairie dog colonies. A study in Colorado reported a year-round average of about four raptors an hour in the air above colonies, with twelve birds an hour at the highest rate observed. Depending on location, some colonies are targeted more frequently than others, but observers have noted that colonies with higher numbers of prairie dogs attract higher concentrations of raptors: more prairie dogs means more potential meals.

Other raptors linked to prairie dog colonies include harriers, rough-legged hawks, snowy owls, kestrels, short-eared owls, and prairie falcons. These smaller raptors do not prey upon prairie dogs (although prairie dog pups are vulnerable), but seek song birds, small mammals — especially rodents — reptiles, amphibians, and the insect life that flourishes there. The less dense vegetation characterizing colonies also benefits the aerial searching and swooping of these birds of prey.

The complex ecosystem that is generated by the colony is characterized to an extreme by another raptor, the burrowing owl. These small owls utilize empty prairie dog burrows for nesting and rely on the mounds for elevation in their hunt for food, consisting mostly of insects and small rodents that are also concentrated in the vicinity.

The vegetation that flourishes around colonies provides food and shelter for other birds as well. Mountain plovers, for example, are highly dependent on prairie dog sites. These birds breed, nest, and feed in these locations because the plant variety and density is ideal for supporting the insects upon which they depend.

In the shortgrass and mixed-grass prairies, bison, antelope, and deer adapt their grazing habits to take advantage of the vegetation that grows in the altered conditions found in prairie dog colonies.

ANIMAL DIVERSITY ASSOCIATED

MAMMALS

badger
bat
black-footed ferret
black-tailed jackrabbit
bobcat
coyote
deer mouse
desert cottontail
eastern cottontail
eastern mole
ground squirrel
hispid pocket mouse
house mouse
kangaroo rat
least chipmunk
long-tailed weasel
mink
northern grasshopper mouse
northern pocket gopher
northern swift fox
Norway rat
olive-backed pocket mouse
Ord's kangaroo rat
plains harvest mouse
plains pocket gopher
porcupine
prairie vole

raccoon
red fox
Richardson's ground squirrel
shrew
silky pocket mouse
southern plains woodrat
spotted ground squirrel
spotted skunk
striped skunk
swift fox

thirteen-lined ground squirrel
western harvest mouse
white-footed mouse
white-tailed cottontail
white-tailed jackrabbit

REPTILES/AMPHIBIANS

bullfrog
bull snake
Chihuahua spotted whiptail
chorus frog

WITH PRAIRIE DOG COLONIES

common garter snake
Couch's spadefoot toad
eastern fence lizard
gopher snake
great plains narrow-mouthed frog
great plains toad
green toad
lesser earless lizard
little spotted whiptail
Mohave rattlesnake
ornate box turtle
plains garter snake
plains spadefoot toad
prairie rattlesnake
racerunner
sagebrush lizard
short-horned lizard
smooth green snake

Texas horned lizard
Texas spotted whiptail
Texas toad

tiger salamander
western box turtle
western chorus frog
western diamondback rattlesnake
western toad
Woodhouse's toad
yellow mud turtle

HERD ANIMALS

bison
elk
mule deer
pronghorn antelope
white-tailed deer

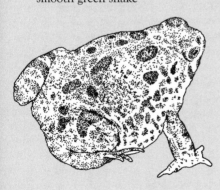

KEYSTONE STATUS

Prairie dogs perform a significant role as a keystone species in grasslands habitat throughout their range, providing shelter for other species and food for predators. Most importantly, their eating habits alter the vegetation, attracting a variety of other animals seeking food.

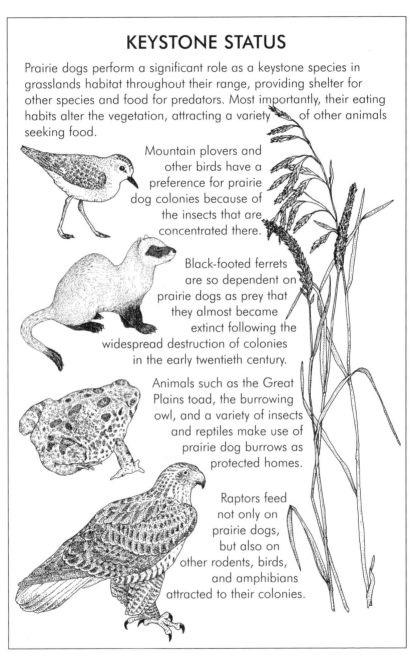

Mountain plovers and other birds have a preference for prairie dog colonies because of the insects that are concentrated there.

Black-footed ferrets are so dependent on prairie dogs as prey that they almost became extinct following the widespread destruction of colonies in the early twentieth century.

Animals such as the Great Plains toad, the burrowing owl, and a variety of insects and reptiles make use of prairie dog burrows as protected homes.

Raptors feed not only on prairie dogs, but also on other rodents, birds, and amphibians attracted to their colonies.

Other plains bird species as well have a strong link to the prairie dog ecosystem. Horned larks, mourning doves, killdeer, barn swallows, and long-billed curlews are among those associated with colony preference over non-colony grasslands. Based on various bird population studies, dozens of other species have a varying degree of association, ranging from strong preference to occasional use.

Larger mammals, too, have an association with prairie dogs. Badgers are a primary predator and not surprisingly, can be found in greater numbers closer to this favorite source of food. They are uniquely equipped to hunt down prairie dogs by digging them out of their burrows. This digging produces enlarged holes and depressions, which can attract other animals and also serve badgers as dens.

Coyotes are another frequent visitor, although prairie dogs are not a major part of their diet. Like raptors, these wild canines gravitate to the prairie dog ecosystem because it provides them with a rich and varied source of prey, from insects and small rodents to ground-dwelling birds. Cottontails are one such prey, and these plains animals are found in much higher concentrations in prairie dog colonies than in the surrounding habitat.

Swift foxes, unlike coyotes, can depend on prairie dogs as a source of food. One study showed that almost 50 percent of their diet consisted of prairie dogs.

The insects that attract birds to this ecosystem are also an attractive source of food for the Great Plains toad. This amphibian makes use of prairie dog burrows for shelter while benefiting from the increase in its food supply in the vicinity. Some species of turtles also make use of the shelter provided by these burrows.

These examples represent some of the characteristics of the ecosystem of prairie dog colonies. While some are clearly dependencies — the burrowing owl, the black-footed ferret, the mountain plover, for example — most vary in importance, being more significant in some seasons or locations than in others.

Yet when considered together, prairie dog colonies assume a

major role for both plants and animals in the grasslands where they are sited. Some scientists believe, in fact, that the prairie dog can be considered a "keystone species," an animal with a wide impact on the environment because of the other life forms it influences.

This is not a universal effect, however. Some animals, such as the grasshopper sparrow, for example, prefer grasslands that are undisturbed by prairie dog colonies. Also, even though the keystone effect is real, it may not apply to every colony. In some individual colonies, for example, the abundance and diversity of bird life may actually be decreased. Further, even though up to two hundred species of animals have been linked to the prairie dog's unique ecosystem, only a few dozen may have a strong dependence, while the connection for the rest ranges from occasional to accidental use.

Overall, however, the prairie dog is unmatched in its role in the grasslands environment. The number and variety of animal life that is affected — in whatever capacity — and the unique aspects of the altered habitat give the prairie dog a powerful position, and supports its status as the most important species in its environment. And even though the plant and animal life associated with these ecosystems can change quickly as colonies come and go, the changes to the soil created by the activity of the prairie dogs can create physical and chemical changes that remain much longer, up to hundreds or thousands of years.

PROFILE OF A NEIGHBOR: BURROWING OWL

"Their hospitality to strangers is unbounded. The owl, who on the bare prairie is unable to find a tree or rock on which to build her nest, is provided with a comfortable lodging, where she may in security rear her round eyed progeny ..."

— Henry Howe (1857, *The Great West*)

Prairie dog colonies provide shelter and ecological support to a number of animal species. One of the most visible is the burrowing owl (*Athene cunicularia*), which uses prairie dog burrows as its preferred nesting site throughout western North America. These ground-dwelling owls are attracted to open spaces, empty burrows that can be used as nesting sites, and the prime hunting territory that is produced by the grazing activity of the prairie dogs. Throughout their range, however, they may also select nesting burrows in rocky crevices or burrows deserted by other animals, including ground squirrels and marmots.

Burrowing owls generally live in harmony with the prairie dogs; these large rodents are not part of their regular diet. Although young prairie dogs and small adults may occasionally be preyed upon by the owls, they live amid the colonies not as a direct predator, but to gain access to their favorite sources of food. Insect prey include grasshoppers, beetles, moths, dragonflies, and crickets; they attack insects on the ground as well as pick them off in the air. Mammal prey includes chipmunks, ground squirrels, mice, rats, shrews, rabbits, bats, and smaller birds. Their diet also includes small amphibians and reptiles.

Although mostly nocturnal, burrowing owls are frequently seen above the ground in daylight hours, perched in their unique long-legged stance atop the mounded entrance to their nests. From this

BURROWING OWL

RANGE
Approximate normal
range of species.

● States where species
is occasionally sighted.

VITAL STATISTICS

NAME	**Burrowing owl** *Athene cunicularia* gopher owl
	FRENCH CANADIAN chouette à terrier SPANISH búho llanero

DESCRIPTION	Small to medium size. Beak pale in color; eyes with yellow pigment. No ear tufts. Body brown in color with distinctive spots; chest and belly white to pale with brown barring. Legs are noticeably longer than other owls. Females and males about the same size.

COMPARISON	Characteristic long legs and activity on ground make this owl distinct from others. In daylight, only small owl perching on ground or in the open.

TOTAL LENGTH	8½–11" (21.6–27.9 cm)	WING LENGTH	6½–7" (16.5–17.8 cm)
WEIGHT	4½–8 oz (120–228 gm)	TAIL LENGTH	3–3½" (7.6–8.9 cm)

RANGE	Year-round resident in southern areas of southwestern states from Pacific coast to Gulf of Mexico. Breeding range includes Sierras east through Rocky Mountains and western plains from southern Canada south to Mexico.

HABITAT	Open, untreed expanses, including mesas, prairies, and plains. Preferred habitat in western range is prairie dog colonies. May visit parks, golf courses.

HABITS	Nocturnal, but perches at entrance to burrow or nearby on low rises in daylight hours. Flies low to ground and uses hovering flight when stalking prey. 6–11 eggs; incubated by females for 21–30 days; 1 brood per year. First flight: 40–45 days.

VOCAL CALL	Chatter notes, "chack, chack, chack ..." and low, quiet "coo-coooo."

vantage point, they are alert to both potential threats and food sources. As they move into burrows that have been dug and abandoned by the prairie dogs, the owls often enlarge and clean these holes with their talons, kicking dirt backward and up to the surface. They line the nesting chamber with a mix of dry material collected in the vicinity, including grasses, twigs, horse and cow dung, feathers, and food debris.

Burrowing owls raise their young as a combined effort by both parents. When the female is incubating the eggs and while the chicks are newly hatched, the male will do most of the hunting, bringing food back to feed the female and young.

One unique characteristic of burrowing owls is their response to threats from predators while they are inside their burrow. Mimicking another frequent resident of the prairies, they produce a distinctive call that sounds like a rattlesnake's rattle. Although rattlesnakes do live in prairie dog burrows, this curious adaptation led to an early myth that both snakes and owls lived together in harmony in the same burrows, which is not the case.

Depending on the availability of food and the presence of other burrowing owls in the vicinity, the size of their territory may range from about one tenth of a square mile to about two square miles (0.25 to 5 square km). In the northern, colder parts of their range, they migrate south during the winter, with some ending up in Central America.

When prairie dogs were common throughout the western states, burrowing owls were also common throughout this range. As habitat destruction and eradication programs have dramatically reduced the traditional range of the prairie dog, so, too, has the natural range of the burrowing owl been affected. Most of the decline occurred in the decades after 1900, when the largest prairie dog eradication efforts were under way, but in the past thirty years, the number of burrowing owls has continued to shrink, about one half percent per year.

Even in areas where prairie dogs are still found, burrowing owls may no longer find enough space to thrive. That is because the new reality for prairie dogs is not only fewer colonies, but smaller colonies. And in many of these smaller colonies, there is not enough open space or empty burrows for the owls. Without enough other owls in a given territory, they cannot find mates.

The smaller colony size of the prairie dogs also produces another negative impact on the burrowing owls. Smaller colonies scattered throughout terrain that has been disrupted by human development provide easier targets for some predators, particularly coyotes, gray foxes, red foxes, and badgers. When more of these predators are around to prey on prairie dogs, burrowing owls may also succumb in greater numbers. In addition, burrowing owls, like many raptors, sometimes scavenge rodents that have been killed by poison, leading to weakness, smaller body sizes, reduced breeding success, and death.

MORTALITY

"The peculiar yelp, like that of a young puppy, seems to be the only reason they are called dogs, for they have nothing else in common with the canine genus. They are not carnivores, but live entirely on grass and roots; they are shaped midway between a squirrel and a ground-hog, have teeth like the former, and belong to the class Rodentia.*"*

— J.H. Beadle (1873, *The Undeveloped West*)

In the wild, prairie dogs may live for several years — up to five years or more. Some individuals have been documented as living up to eight years. In captivity, there are reports of individuals living up to ten years. Most deaths occur during the first year, when babies and young pups are vulnerable to predators, cannibalism, disease, and lack of food.

Prairie dogs groom themselves frequently and live in relatively clean conditions. But even so, their short, dense fur, the tightly knit social groups in which they live, and the prime insect breeding grounds represented by their burrows make them targets for a number of parasites, especially fleas, mites, and ticks.

Tularemia, also known as rabbit fever, is a disease caused by a bacterium called *Francisella tularensis*, which periodically affects prairie dogs. Humans have been known to contract *blastomycosis*, a respiratory illness, from prairie dog colonies. The disease does not come directly from the animals, however, but from fungal spores that can reside in the soil there.

Fleas are the major threat to prairie dogs and are a constant presence for all species throughout North America. Fleas have evolved to specialize in host animals after thousands of years of co-habitation, and certain flea species make prairie dogs their only host. These fleas often harbor diseases such as plague. At frequent intervals, outbreaks of the plague will erupt and turn into a localized epidemic, fully capable of wiping out the entire population of a colony. Even when not

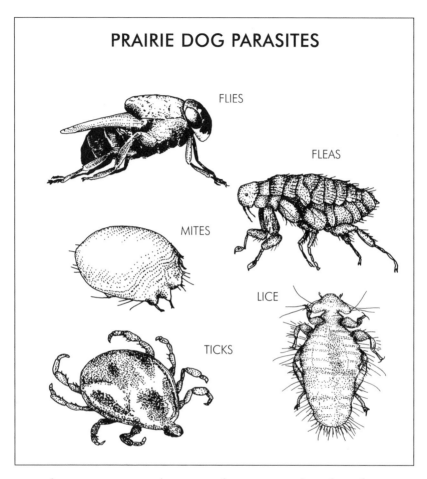

PRAIRIE DOG PARASITES

FLIES

FLEAS

MITES

LICE

TICKS

at epidemic proportions, however, plague is now thought to be a permanent threat. The plague is also a threat to humans who come into contact with prairie dogs, or in some cases, who just get close enough to attract plague-carrying fleas. In modern times, throughout their current range, numerous cases have been reported of human beings contracting this disease. A few deaths have also been reported.

The plague that infects prairie dogs is technically referred to as sylvatic plague, caused by a specific kind of bacterium, *Yersinia pestis*, and is carried by fleas. Sylvatic plague can be carried by many different kinds of mammals, but is mostly linked to rodents, including deer mice and kangaroo rats. These smaller rodents can carry the disease without being affected by any symptoms; in prairie dogs, however, it is almost 100 percent fatal.

Biologists theorize that this plague was not native to North America, but arrived with western settlement. One of the first observations of its effects on wild rodents was in 1908 near San Francisco. Since then, it has spread throughout most of the western states and the Great Plains.

When plague first sweeps into an area, individual prairie dogs are quickly infected and die. Often, entire coteries and colonies succumb to its effects, sometimes depressing the population in an area too low to rebound, leading to local extinction. Despite this threat, some areas within the normal range of the prairie dog have not been infected, but an estimated 66 percent of the total current range is thought to be affected.

Some biologists also believe that widespread poisoning — resulting in large expanses of territory with no colonies present — has created effective barriers that may help prevent or slow future spread of this disease. Although prairie dogs are often the victim of the plague, they are not thought to be carriers because they are so susceptible, dying before they have a chance to pass it on.

Fleas pick up the plague bacterium when they bite animals that carry it. Later, when they bite another animal, the bacterium is passed on, but the disease can also be passed directly from one infected mammal to another during certain infectious stages. Plague is often referred to as bubonic plague, pneumonic plague, and septicemic plague; these terms are linked to specific forms as they affect different parts of the body.

Although fleas are the prime carrier of plague in prairie dog colonies, and most prairie dogs have fleas most of the time, few flea species are actually carriers. Also, those flea species that co-exist with prairie dogs prefer these and other animals to human beings, reducing the chance that a person might be infected because a flea

PRAIRIE DOGS AND FLEAS

Fleas are a major parasite for most rodents, including prairie dogs, because of their unique life cycle. After feeding off the blood of its host, a female flea deposits egg cases in the rodent's nesting chamber. Upon hatching, the larvae feed on organic debris and eventually produce cocoons, turning into pupae. Pupae grow through several stages and may hatch into adults in about one week. However, they can also survive for a year or more if rodents are not present; hatching depends on the presence of rodents. Adult fleas can live for several years, constantly feeding on their hosts and reproducing. But they are also able to live for up to several months without feeding if no rodent — and the blood they provide — is available.

ADULT FLEA

EGG CASE

LARVA

PUPAL STAGES

Several species of fleas are adapted to living primarily on prairie dogs, but these species and those found mostly on other rodents may transfer from one animal to another during some circumstances. Diseases such as plague can be transmitted during such transfers.

abandoned its host, attracted to a new warm body. And since infected prairie dogs die quickly, it is very unlikely that people could get plague directly from them without the fleas as intermediaries.

In most cases, dogs that come into contact with plague-infested fleas or other infested animals do not contract the disease themselves. Cats, on the other hand, are extremely vulnerable but in North America, there are not many known cases of the disease. Dogs and cats, however, can spread the disease to people through infected fleas as well as direct contact, such as coughing or sneezing.

As the plague in prairie dog colonies moved eastward from its first observance in 1908, human cases of the disease also shifted in that direction. In Oregon, the first case was reported in 1934; someone was infected in Utah in 1936; it hit Nevada in 1937; Idaho in 1940, New Mexico in 1949, and reached Colorado in 1957. Cases have also been observed in Nevada, Montana, Texas, Arizona, Wyoming, Montana, and Washington. Only South Dakota has remained plague-free to date, but outbreaks have been noted on its borders.

Once plague has been introduced to an area, biologists believe that it remains there, passing among host animals whether or not any show signs of infection. With prairie dog colonies, an eruption of the disease may wipe out most or all of a colony or group of colonies and appear again years later after the population has begun to recover. Studies of plague-affected colonies indicate that, although the surviving animals may breed quickly and take advantage of less population density to expand faster, the total population rarely, if ever, comes back to its former level. It is estimated to take four to five years for a colony to recuperate from a plague attack, but because the disease may still linger in the area, quietly "hiding" in other animals, it is poised to strike again with similar devastating results.

Gunnison prairie dogs have been affected more than most other species, not in total numbers, but overall effect. Since the first plague cases were reported among this species in 1945, the total territory occupied by these animals declined to about 5 percent of its previous area, with 67 percent of the lost acres due to plague deaths. Of the total acreage occupied by black-tailed prairie dogs in Montana in the 1980s, about 50 percent had been lost by the 1990s because of the impact of plague on colonies there.

One study of the incidence of plague in humans in the United States has shown that only 13 percent of the cases reported were related to contact with prairie dogs or to the fleas they are associated with. Between 1994 and 1998, there were forty cases of plague reported in humans in the Unites States, of which only nine were definitively connected to prairie dogs.

When prairie dog colonies are hit with an outbreak of the plague, it often wipes them out. If any individuals do survive, biologists believe that it is an accident of avoidance, because no prairie dogs have been shown to produce antibodies or other evidence of immunity after exposure.

How can you tell if a prairie dog colony is infected with plague? As a general rule of thumb, if there are prairie dogs visible and active, there's no plague. Colonies hit with this disease collapse within a few days, with most or all of the members dead. Still, it is never wise to be close to any rodents in the western states because this threat exists, as well as other dangerous diseases such as hantavirus.

To minimize any potential threat when close to prairie dog colonies, visitors should not attempt to feed animals, no matter how cute, appealing, and tame they appear. Walking through colonies is also not wise. For visitors with dogs, leashes are a must, as much to protect the dogs from fleas as the prairie dogs from harassment.

CONSERVATION

"Over most of this extensive scope of country the prairie-dog is no longer a factor to be reckoned with by the farmer and stockman. To such an extent has the little animal become a thing of the past in many localities that the occasional isolated 'dog-town' is now looked upon by the residents as a matter of interest and old-time association rather than as a nuisance."

— Theo. H. Scheffer (1909, Kansas State Agricultural College Circular Number 4)

In a few places throughout their range in recent years, prairie dogs are so numerous that they are a nuisance, at least to some landowners. But despite this problem, their numbers are so reduced from their original population size that conservation efforts are under way to protect remaining colonies. And even though poisoning and other eradication efforts are still legal and promoted throughout most of their remaining range, public and scientific interest is now beginning to shift.

In the early 1900s, before widespread ranching and farming — not to mention urbanization — had a significant effect, as many as five billion black-tailed prairie dogs are thought to have occupied their original range. Prairie dogs did not fare well in the face of competition from ranchers and farmers moving into prime land west of the Missouri River. As early as 1902, scientific studies sponsored by federal and state agriculture departments reported that prairie dogs posed a serious threat to the food supply for cattle, reducing grasses and other edible vegetation from 50 to 75 percent.

This kind of authoritative conclusion triggered the widespread development of eradication programs designed to eliminate prairie dogs and thus leave more vegetation for livestock grazing. In recent years, more advanced research has determined that prairie dogs exert less than 10 percent negative competition on existing vegetation.

A number of control methods were proposed and implemented, but poisoning was the only program that had immediate and effective results. Some of these methods involved direct application of chemicals in burrows and surrounding terrain; some poisons were applied to oats or other attractive food baits, which were scattered within colonies.

Poison is still a regular part of the arsenal deployed against these "agricultural pests," but increasing amounts of territory have been shifted to a protective status. These days, the biggest enemy from the human front is not ranchers or agriculture in general, but urban sprawl. Shopping centers, industrial parks, highways, parking lots, and residential developments are expanding throughout most of the territory that prairie dogs originally called home. And even when progressive protection policies are in place, prairie dogs often acquire the label of unwanted pest in the face of profitable urban sprawl.

Very few urbanization schemes have been stopped or altered by the presence of prairie dog colonies, although more and more are delayed while solutions are sought. Increasingly, this means relocation, with specialized teams of wildlife professionals and wildlife-loving amateurs trapping and removing unwanted colonies.

The method of choice for trapping is water, the same method used by Lewis and Clark when they first encountered a prairie dog burrow. Using hoses connected to tanker trucks or hydrants, burrows are flooded with water, forcing their inhabitants to surface, where they are placed in cages for transporting to a new location. One alternative to water is a giant vacuum hose, successfully used to suck the rodents from their burrows.

Metropolitan areas where prairie dog colonies exist have discovered these animals help attract visitors and support "watchable wildlife" interests. But colonies surrounded by developments can also pose ongoing problems. As prairie dog families expand and new members push up the population, the pressure is on for some animals to seek new territory. Driven by instinct and the need to establish new family groups, expanding prairie dog towns can push into

143

PRAIRIE DOG CONSERVATION

ARIZONA
There are no black-tailed colonies remaining in the state.

COLORADO
State regulations list prairie dogs as "destructive rodent pests" and they are considered an agricultural nuisance. Counties have the right to eradicate colonies and the animals are not permitted to be live-trapped and transported from one county to another without permission. Licensed hunters can shoot prairie dogs without restriction.

IDAHO
Information unavailable.

KANSAS
Although the state lists prairie dogs as wildlife, they are also officially designated as an agricultural pest. Licensed hunters are permitted to shoot them year-round without restriction. Prairie dogs that move from one piece of private land to another may also be eradicated.

MONTANA
State agencies classify prairie dogs as "vertebrate pests," and suppression programs are regularly carried out; hunting is permitted.

NEBRASKA
State law defines prairie dogs as a nongame species that is unprotected, permitting killing or control by any method. Licensed hunters are also allowed to shoot them.

NEW MEXICO
Listed as a "rodent pest," prairie dogs are expected to be killed by private landowners after notification by the state. The state can also perform this task, billing landowners for the activity. State regulations also permit unrestricted hunting of prairie dogs by licensed hunters.

STATUS STATE-BY-STATE

NORTH DAKOTA

The state lists prairie dogs as pests and authorizes extermination, even on private land. Counties and townships are also permitted to issue bounties for prairie dog extermination when private landowners fail to kill them after notification.

OKLAHOMA

Hunting prairie dogs in this state requires only a license; no restrictions are placed on numbers. State agencies can assist landowners in controlling prairie dogs that are considered a problem.

SOUTH DAKOTA

State control programs manage prairie dog colonies that are considered a threat to public health, livestock, or game. Landowners are also granted poisoning rights as prairie dogs are classified as an agricultural pest in the state; colonies on private land must be at least 100 yards from adjoining property. State authorities can also go onto private land in order to exterminate colonies. Licensed hunters are permitted to shoot unrestricted numbers.

TEXAS

State regulations classify prairie dogs as a public nuisance and local programs assist landowners in poisoning colonies. Licensed hunters are permitted unrestricted numbers.

UTAH

Poisoning is permitted if prairie dogs are determined to be a pest on private agricultural land.

WYOMING

Prairie dogs are designated as pests and a state program permits officials to enter private land to inspect for the presence of the animals. Control of prairie dog colonies on private land is required, with fines for failure to cooperate. Hunting in unrestricted numbers is allowed.

golf courses, highway medians, cemeteries, parks, and private lawns. One solution may be the use of birth control chemicals to reduce the population expansion. Some western cities also rely on population reduction, by removing some individuals for relocation when over-population generates problems.

While prairie dogs may be a pest in some areas, the fact that their overall population has been reduced to only 1 percent of its original size is of great concern to biologists. Most of the eradication programs that targeted prairie dogs had their greatest effect in the first half of the 1900s, but population declines among the remaining colonies continue. If prairie dog numbers continue to decrease, it is likely that one or more of the species may no longer be able to maintain a healthy mix of genes, leading eventually to extinction. This potential outcome is helping foster conservation programs now, before the declines are too great to reverse.

To conservationists and ecologists, the prairie dog is considered a keystone species. Such an animal is considered a significant presence in an environmental area, representing complex interactions with many other plant and animals species. A keystone species can indicate healthy, normal ecological conditions as well as declining ecological health. Certain other animal species are threatened by future declines in the prairie dog population. The black-footed ferret is the most notorious example, now an official endangered species. Others linked to prairie dog colonies include the mountain plover, a bird that relies heavily on this habitat for its breeding, nesting, and feeding activity. Currently the mountain plover is a candidate to become an endangered species. The ferruginous hawk also depends on this habitat and the prairie dog itself as a major source of food. This hawk is now listed as a "sensitive" species, one that is in danger of decline. The western burrowing owl is another raptor listed as sensitive, also closely linked to prairie dog colonies for its nesting and feeding activity. The swift fox is a candidate to be listed as endangered. This small predator depends heavily on the short grass habitat and prairie dog colonies for its stalking and feeding activity.

When visitors first began traveling through the American West, they often encountered prairie dog colonies that stretched for miles and contained populations numbering in the hundreds of thousands. This illustration is captioned, "A Town, in Nebraska, of Prairie Dogs," from *Historical Collections of the Great West*, by Henry Howe, published in 1857.

The original population of prairie dogs in North America stretched across thousands of miles and provided numerous opportunities for genetic distribution. As this population has shrunk, it has resulted in small groups living in isolation, unable to benefit from the same wide genetic mix. This kind of fragmentation, despite short-term survival success in some parts of their range, may be the greatest long-term threat to the survival of this animal.

PEST CONTROL

"The prairie dogs are making terrible havoc on corn and wheat fields in our immediate neighborhood. The farmers have waged war on them and say they intend to drive them away."

— Saline County Journal (Kansas), June 12, 1879

Despite the fact that prairie dogs are endangered or threatened throughout much of their range, government rules still permit them to be hunted, poisoned, and eradicated in some areas. In a few parts of their remaining range, this activity has gradually shifted toward relocation rather than eradication, but not without problems. For one thing, live trapping and moving prairie dogs costs a lot more than killing them, and before they can be relocated, appropriate locations have to be selected for their release, which is not a simple task.

Control by poisoning also has drawbacks. Colonies that have been eliminated by poison may be quickly repopulated by prairie dogs migrating in from nearby colonies. Plus, even with careful use, poisons and poisoned baits used in these efforts are often eaten by other animals, compounding the killing.

Removing prairie dogs by live trapping is likely to become the only appropriate solution in locations where they represent a problem. But some studies suggest there may be other options. Visual barriers, for instance, have proven effective in keeping prairie dogs from expanding outside already established sites. In use, these barriers — low curtains made of fabric or other materials — prevent prairie dogs from seeing other places to go. Just as with natural barriers of tall vegetation where they cannot see well enough to spot predators, they are unwilling to venture.

These barriers only work when they are completely outside of the range of underground burrows, otherwise, the animals can bypass the barriers by traveling below them. Holes in the barrier that admit even small amounts of light — within the span or at the bottom edge — have proven to be a problem with this technique, as appearance of light triggers the animals to claw and chew through the blocking material. Heights of about four feet have proven ideal to create a natural blockade. To be effective, such barriers also need to have a bottom edge that is buried to a depth of several inches to prevent light from leaking through. Some barrier designs also include an electrified wire, thought to be especially effective at controlling prairie dog movement away from a colony.

The same barrier effect can be achieved with natural vegetation, at least in some locations. Prairie dogs in the wild generally avoid territory where tall grasses or brush flourish. Their original range, in fact, was limited to short and mixed-grass prairies, ending near the Missouri River, where traditional tall grass prairies extended to the east. In places where domestic cattle were introduced, however, these bovines altered the ecosystem by reducing the height of vegetation as they foraged on the native tall grasses. In response, prairie dog colonies often appeared to take advantage of the newly advantageous conditions.

Experiments conducted in western Nebraska suggest that the natural habit of prairie dogs to avoid tall grasses can be used to help control the outward growth of their colonies. In practice, cattle grazing in some areas has been deferred during the prime spring and summer growing months. In response, tall grasses grew at a faster rate than prairie dogs could control, decreasing the population of some colonies through lower birth rates and reducing the overall size of some colonies.

In general, when prairie dogs are trapped and relocated, they have a greater chance of survival as a group. In some studies, groups of ten animals had a low survival and reproductive rate in their new location, a factor related to this animal's instinctive dependence on group behavior to protect itself against predators. When relocated groups numbered sixty or more, on the other hand, they tend to survive better and even expand in numbers over time.

PRAIRIE DOGS AS PETS

"He is very soon reconciled to a state of captivity, and after two days appears on the most intimate terms with his captors. Even when turned loose again the creatures will not leave the neighbourhood of the house, but burrow under the foundation, making themselves quite at home, and fearlessly come out to be fed when summoned by a whistle. They become, indeed, very interesting and pretty little pets."

— William H.G. Kingston (1884, *The Western World*)

Small, cute, and cuddly, prairie dogs have attracted human interest as pets for more than one hundred years. In recent years, this interest has blossomed into a mini-industry, with prairie dog breeders raising young animals for sale in the pet market, both in North America and overseas, particularly in Japan. There may be as many as tens of thousands of young animals sold annually as part of this trend.

Although some species of prairie dog are endangered and their numbers are greatly reduced from historical highs, it is unlikely that demand from the pet industry will have a serious effect on their survival in the wild. But there are also other issues involved with the pet concept, particularly the quality of life of transplanted wildlife being raised to bond with humans. As with birds and other small mammals, the greatest value that humans can place on wild creatures is to observe and enjoy them in the wild, not transplant them into an alien environment where the interaction has been altered to suit the pet owner.

PRAIRIE DOG WATCHING

Throughout most of their natural range, prairie dogs have largely disappeared, the result of widespread poisoning and the effects of the plague. These communal rodents still exist in isolated pockets, however, and in some cases protected within the confines of state and federal parks and wildlife preserves. The following list includes some of the sites where the public may enjoy observing the activities of this native animal. When close to wild animals, observers should always remember some basic guidelines. Prairie dogs, however cute, are still wild. Like all animals in the wild, they do not need to be fed and even if used to people, should not be petted or touched. When visiting prairie dog colonies with domestic dogs, keep them on leash.

ARIZONA

Anderson Mesa/Coconino National Forest
2323 East Greenlaw Lane
Flagstaff, AZ 86004
520-527-3600
www.fs.fed.us/r3/coconino

Arizona-Sonora Desert Museum
2021 N. Kinney Road
Tucson, AZ 85743-8918
520-883-1380
www.desertmuseum.org

Petrified Forest National Park
P.O. Box 2217
Petrified Forest National Park,
   AZ 86028
928-524-6228
www.nps.gov/pefo

COLORADO

Comanche National Grasslands
27204 Highway 287
Springfield, CO 81073
719-523-6591
www.fs.fed.us/r2/psicc/coma

Navajo State Park
P.O. Box 1697
1526 County Road 982
Arboles, CO 81121
970-883-2208
www.coloradoparks.org

Pawnee National Grasslands
660 O Street
Greeley, CO 80631
907-353-5004
www.fs.fed.us/r2/arnf/png

KANSAS

Cimarron National Grasslands
242 East Highway 56
Elkhart, Kansas 67950
620-697-4621
www.fs.fed.us/r2/psicc/cim

Fort Larned City Park
Fort Larned, Kansas

Kanopolis State Park/Kanopolis Wildlife Area
200 Horsethief Road
Marquette, KS 67456
785-546-2565

Prairie Dog State Park
Box 43
Norton, Kansas 67654
785-877-2953

Quivira National Wildlife Refuge
Route 3, Box 48A
Stafford, KS 67578
316-486-2393

Smokey Valley Ranch
The Nature Conservancy
785-233-4400

MONTANA

Charles M. Russell National Wildlife Refuge
Lewistown, MT 59457
406-538-8706
www.r6.fws.gov/cmr

Glacier National Park
West Glacier, MT 59936
406-888-7800
www.nps.gov/glac

Greycliffe Prairie Dog Town State Park
2300 Lake Elmo Drive
Billings, MT 59105
307-406-2940

Ulm Pishkun State Park
342 Ulm-Vaughn Road
Ulm, MT 59485
406-866-2217

Upper Missouri River Breaks National Monument
Airport Road Box 1160
Lewistown, MT 59457
406-538-7461
www.mt.blm.gov/ldo/um/
    um_general.html

NEBRASKA

Fort Niobrara National Wildlife Refuge
Hidden Timer Route,
    HC 14, Box 67
Valentine, NE 69201
402-376-3789
www.r6.fws.gov/refuges/niobrara/
    niobrara.htm

152

National Grasslands Visitor's Center
708 Main Street
Wall, SD 57790
605-279-2125
www.fs.fed.us/r2/nebraska/units/
    frrd/ngvisitor.html

Oglala National Grassland
16524 Highway 385
Chadron, NE 69337
308-432-4475

The City of Santa Fe has a captive colony in the municipal park.

Kiowa/Rita Blanca National Grassland
714 Main Street
Clayton, NM 88415
505-374-9652

Maxwell National Wildlife Refuge
P.O. Box 276
Maxwell, NM 87728
505-375-2331

Vermejo Park Ranch
P.O. Drawer E
Raton, NM 87740
505-445-3097
www.vermejoparkranch.com

Arrowwood National Wildlife Refuge
7745 11th Street SE
Pingree, ND 58476-8308
701-285-3341

Cheyenne National Grassland
Box 946
Lisbon, ND 58054
701-683-4342

Little Missouri National Grassland
161 21st Street West
Dickinson, ND 58601
701-225-5151

Sullys Hill National Game Preserve (south of Devils Lake)
701-766-4272
www.r6.fws.gov/refuges/sullys

Theodore Roosevelt National Park, South Unit
P.O. Box 7
Medora, North Dakota 58645
www.nps.gov/thro/home.htm

Wichita Mountains National Wildlife Refuge
Route 1, Box 448
Indiahoma, OK 73552
580-429-3221
//southwest.fws.gov/refuges/
    oklahoma/Wichita/
    wmwrhome.html

McClellan Creek/Black Kettle
National Grasslands
Box 55B, Route 1
Cheyenne, OK 73628
580-497-2143

Buffalo Gap National Grassland
209 North River
Hot Springs, SD 57747
605-745-4107

Cedar River/Grand River
National Grasslands
1005 5th Avenue West
Lemmon, SD 57638
605-374-3592

Fort Pierre National Grassland
24 South Euclid Avenue
Pierre, SD 57501
605-224-5517

Lacreek National Wildlife
Refuge
HWC 3, Box 14
Martin, SD 57551
605-685-6508

Buffalo Lake National
Wildlife Refuge
P.O. Box 179
Umbarger, TX 79091
806-499-3382

Lyndon B. Johnson/Caddo
National Grasslands
1400 North U.S. 81/287 Highway
Decatur, TX 76234
940-627-5475

Muleshoe National Wildlife
Refuge
P.O. Box 549
Muleshoe, TX 79347
806-946-3341

Rita Blanca National Grassland
714 Main Street
Clayton, NM 88415
505-374-9652
www.fs.fed.us/r3/cibola/
   district_files/d7.htm

Canyonlands National Park
2282 South West Resource Blvd.
Moab, UT 84532-3298
435-719-2313
www.nps.gov/cany

Desert Lake Waterfowl
Management Area
(near Huntington)
Utah Department of Wildlife
435-637-3310

Fish Lake Basin (near Loa)
U.S. Forest Service
435-836-2811

Ouray National Wildlife Refuge
1680 West Highway 40, 112-C
Vernal, UT 84078
801-789-0351

Thunder Basin National Grassland/Medicine Bow-Routt National Forest
2468 Jackson Street
Laramie, WY 82070
307-745-2300
www.fs.fed.us/mrnf

Devils Tower National Monument
P.O. Box 10
Devils Tower, WY 82714-0010
307-467-5283
www.nps.gov/deto/home.htm

Fossil Butte National Monument
P.O. Box 592
Kemmerer, WY 83101
307-877-4455
www.nps.gov/fobu

Seedskadee National Wildlife Refuge
P.O. Box 700
Green River, WY 82935
307-875-2187

Grasslands National Park
P.O. Box 150
Val Marie, Saskatchewan
Canada S0N 2T0
306-298-2257
//parkscanada.pch.gc.ca/parks/
   saskatchewan/grasslands/
   grasslands_e.htm

RESOURCES

Black-footed Ferret Recovery Program
www.blackfootedferret.org

Canadian Wildlife Federation
2740 Queensview Drive
Ottawa, Ontario K2B 1A2 Canada
www.cwf-fcf.org

Canadian Wildlife Service
351 St. Joseph Blvd.
Hull, Quebec K1A 0H3 Canada
819-997-1095
www.cws-scf.ec.gc.ca

Defenders of Wildlife
1101 14th Street NW, Suite 1400
Washington, DC 20005
202-682-9400
www.defenders.org

Forest Service/USDA
201 14th Street SW
Washington, DC 20024
202-205-1103
www.fs.fed.us

Friends of the Earth
1025 Vermont Ave. NW
Washington, DC 20005
202-783-7400
www.foe.org

Great Plains Restoration Council
P.O. Box 46216
Denver, CO 46216
303-573-6569
www.gprc.org

Humane Society of the U.S.
2100 L Street NW
Washington, DC 20037
202-452-1100
www.hsus.org

International Wildlife Education & Conservation
237 Hill Street
Santa Monica, CA 90405
310-392-6257
www.iwec.org

National Audubon Society
700 Broadway
New York, NY 10003
212-979-3000
www.audubon.org

National Park Service
1849 C Street NW
Washington, DC 20240
202-208-6843
www.nps.gov

National Wildlife Federation
8925 Leesburg Pike
Vienna, VA 22184
703-790-4000
www.nwf.org

National Wildlife Research Center
USDA Wildlife Services
4101 LaPorte Ave.
Fort Collins, CO 80521
970-266-6000
www.aphis.usda.gov/ws/nwrc

The Nature Conservancy
4245 North Fairfax Drive, Suite 100
Arlington, VA 22203
800-628-6860
www.tnc.org

Prairie Ecosystem Conservation Alliance
P.O. Box 370264
Denver, CO 80237-0264
303-338-0567

Predator Conservation Alliance
P.O. Box 6733
Bozeman, Montana 59771
406-587-3389
www.predatorconservation.org

Save the Prairie Dogs
Rocky Mountain Animal Defense
2525 Arapahoe #E4-335
Boulder, CO 80302
720-565-9096
www.prairiedogs.org

Sierra Club
85 2nd Street, 2nd Floor
San Francisco, CA 94109
415-977-5500
www.sierraclub.org

Southern Plains Land Trust
P.O. Box 66
Pritchett, CO 81064
719-523-6296
www.southernplains.org

U.S. Fish and Wildlife Service
1849 C Street NW
Washington, DC 20240
202-208-3100
www.fws.gov

The Wilderness Society
900 17th Street NW
Washington, DC 20006
202-833-2300
www.wilderness.org

Wildlife Services Program/USDA
4700 River Road
Riverdale, MD 20737-1236
301-734-3256
www.aphis.usda.gov/ws

The Wildlife Society
5410 Grosvenor Lane, Suite 200
Bethesda, MD 20814
301-897-9770
www.wildlife.org

Wildlife 2000
P.O. Box 6428
Denver, CO 80206
303-333-8294

World Wildlife Fund
1250 24th Street NW
Washington, DC 20037
202-293-4800
www.worldwildlife.org

World Wildlife Fund Canada
245 Eglinton Ave. East, Suite 410
Toronto, Ontario M4P 3J1 Canada
416-489-8800
www.wwfcanada.org

BIBLIOGRAPHY

Agnew, William. *Flora and Fauna Associated with Prairie Dog Ecosystems.* 1983, thesis, Colorado State University.

Armstrong, David M. *Rocky Mountain Mammals.* 1975, Rocky Mountain Nature Association and the National Park Service.

Bailey, Vernon. *Mammals of the Southwestern United States.* 1971, Dover Publications. Originally published in 1931 as Mammals of New Mexico, by the United States Department of Agriculture Bureau of Biological Survey.

Benyus, Janine M. *The Field Guide to Wildlife Habitats of the Western United States.* 1989, Fireside Books/Simon & Schuster.

Brown, Lauren. *Grasslands.* 1998, National Audubon Society Nature Guides/Alfred A. Knopf.

Burt, William Henry. *A Field Guide to the Mammals: North America North of Mexico* (Third Edition). 1980, Peterson Field Guide Series/Houghton Mifflin Company.

Cincotta, Paul. *Habitat and Dispersal of Black-Tailed Prairie Dogs in Badlands National Park.* 1985, dissertation, Colorado State University.

Clark, Tim W. *Ecology and Ethology of the White-Tailed Prairie Dog.* 1977, Milwaukee Public Museum Press.

Coppock, David Layne. *Impacts of Black-Tailed Prairie Dogs on Vegetation in Wind Cave National Park.* 1981, thesis, Colorado State University.

Cushing, Frank Hamilton. *Zuñi Folk Tales.* 1901, G.P. Putnam's Sons.

Dary, David A. *The Buffalo Book: The Full Saga of the American Animal.* 1974, Swallow Press/Ohio University Press.

Dorsey, George A. *The Pawnee: Mythology.* 1906, Carnegie Institution of Washington. Republished in 1997 by University of Nebraska Press.

Fleharty, Eugene D. *Wild Animals and Settlers on the Great Plains.* 1995, University of Oklahoma Press.

Forrest, Louise R. *Field Guide to Tracking Animals in Snow.* 1988, Stackpole Books.

Hadidian, John; Hodge, Guy; and Grandy, John W. *Wild Neighbors: The Humane Approach to Living with Wildlife.* 1997, Fulcrum Publishing and the Humane Society of the United States.

Halfpenny, James. *A Field Guide to Mammal Tracking in North America.* 1986, Johnson Books.

Hengesbaugh, Mark Gerard. *Creatures of Habit: The Changing Nature of Wildlife and Wild Place in Utah and the Intermountain West*. 2001, Utah State University Press.

Hoogland, John L. *The Black-Tailed Prairie Dog*. 1995, University of Chicago Press.

King, John A. *Social Behavior, Social Organization, and Population Dynamics in a Black-Tailed Prairie Dog Town in the Black Hills of South Dakota*. 1955, Contributions from the Laboratory of Vertebrate Biology/University of Michigan.

Lawrence, R.D. *Owls: The Silent Fliers*. 1997, Firefly Books.

Martin, Alexander C., Zim, Herbert S., and Nelson, Arnold L. *American Wildlife and Plants: A Guide to Wildlife Food Habits*. 1951, McGraw-Hill Book Company, Inc. Republished in 1961 by Dover Publications.

Miller, Brian; Reading, Richard P.; and Forrest, Steve. *Prairie Night: Black-Footed Ferrets and the Recovery of Endangered Species*. 1996, Smithsonian Institution Press.

Murie, Jan O., and Michener, Gail R. *The Biology of Ground-Dwelling Squirrels*. 1984, University of Nebraska Press.

Nelson, Edward W. *Wild Animals of North America: Intimate Studies of Big and Little Creatures of the Mammal Kingdom*. 1918, National Geographic Society.

Nowak, Ronald M. *Walker's Mammals of the World*, Sixth Edition. 1999, Johns Hopkins University Press.

Oldemeyer, John L.; Biggins, Deane; Miller, Brian J.; and Crete, Ronald, editors. *Proceedings of the Symposium on the Management of the Prairie Dog Complexes for the Reintroduction of the Black-Footed Ferret*. 1993, Fish and Wildlife Service/U.S. Department of the Interior.

Olin, George. *Mammals of the Southwest Mountains and Mesas*. 1961, Southwestern Parks and Monuments Association.

Pizzimenti, John J. *Evolution of the Prairie Dog Genus Cynomys*. 1975, Museum of Natural History and Department of Systematics and Ecology, The University of Kansas.

Rand, A. L. *Mammals of the Eastern Rockies and Western Plains of Canada*. 1948, National Museum of Canada.

Riley, Laura, and Riley, William. *Guide to the National Wildlife Refuges*. 1992, Macmillan.

Rockwell, David. *The Nature of North America: A Handbook to the Continent, Rocks, Plants, and Animals*. 1998, Berkley Books.

Rue, Leonard Lee, III. *Sportsman's Guide to Game Animals: A Field Book of North American Species*. 1968, Outdoor Life Books/Harper & Row.

Seton, Ernest Thompson. *Wild Animals at Home*. 1913, Grosset & Dunlap.

Smith, Ronald E. *Natural History of the Prairie Dog in Kansas*. 1967, Museum of Natural History and State Biological Survey/University of Kansas.

Tileston, Jules V. *Comparison of a White-Tailed Prairie Dog Town with a Black-Tailed Prairie Dog Town in North-Central Colorado*. 1961, thesis, Colorado State University.

Van Gelder, Richard G. *Mammals of the National Parks*. 1982, Johns Hopkins University Press.

Van Pelt, William E., editor. *The Black-Tailed Prairie Dog, Conservation Assessment and Strategy*. 1999, Mountain and Prairie Division/U.S. Fish and Wildlife Service.

Wade, Kevin. *Black-Tailed Prairie Dog Management: Translocation and Barriers*. 1992, thesis, Colorado State University.

Whitaker, John O., Jr. *National Audubon Society Field Guide to North American Mammals*. 1980, Alfred A. Knopf.

Wolfe, David W. *Tales From the Underground: A Natural History of Subterranean Life*. 2001, Perseus Publishing.

Wright, N. Pelham. *A Guide to Mexican Animals*. 1965, Minutiae Mexicana.

Zeveloff, Samuel I. *Mammals of the Intermountain West*. 1988, University of Utah Press.

INDEX

Other Titles in the Johnson Nature Series

Squirrels: A Wildlife Handbook
ISBN 1-55566-152-1

Owls: A Wildlife Handbook
ISBN 1-55566-200-5

Hummingbirds: A Wildlife Handbook
ISBN 1-55566-188-2

Beavers: A Wildlife Handbook
ISBN 1-55566-251-X

Wolves: A Wildlife Handbook
ISBN 1-55566-158-0

Frogs: A Wildlife Handbook
ISBN 1-55566-226-9